Once again, Dr Mary O'Kane has delivered a must-read manual for parents struggling to understand and support their anxious children. Delivered in her trademark no nonsense, easy to digest and empathetic style, parents will feel empowered and educated with this book as their guide. Practical & interesting, Mary uses science, psychology, and real-life experience to illustrate that parents do indeed have the power to help their children successfully navigate life in an anxious world. This book will put your parental mind at ease.

Karen Koster, Broadcaster

In a world gripped by heightened parental anxiety 'Anxious Children in an Anxious World' shines as an indispensable toolkit. This book not only addresses the unique challenges children face but also provides practical and effective strategies for parents to navigate their own anxieties. In an era where concerns are magnified, this book stands out, offering both solace and actionable guidance for those navigating the intricate landscape of raising children amidst pervasive anxiety. A must-read for parents seeking support in these challenging times.

Tommy Bowe, Former Rugby Player and Ireland AM Presenter

I devoured this book. Not because I have any particularly anxious children but because Mary's writing explains so much about kids in general. The structure of the book is great. The Give It a Try! sections are particularly helpful and the From the Horse's Mouth pieces make you relate to Mary even more as a human. The message that we, as parents, don't need to be perfect and that we don't need to raise perfect children is so empowering.

Dave Moore, Today FM

Once again Mary has created an incredibly valuable resource for parents. In this book she helps us to navigate periods of anxiety our children may experience and anxious thoughts they may have. She has given us the tools to better understand what anxiety is, how it can manifest itself and ways to live with it. One chapter

I found really resonated with me was Resilience and Risk. I took a lot away from this chapter I am committed to putting into practice. Mary has presented this book into easily digestible chapters with helpful boxes of information from the experts, top tips and practice exercises to do with kids to help them cope with anxiety.

Alison Curtis, Weekend Breakfast on Today FM

This book does exactly what it says in the title. It is filled with hope that you can work through and help your child face anxiety. It gives you the parent tangible tools to use in the moment that are practical, evidence-based, effective, human and warm. Helping you and your child know that anxious kids are brave every day, Dr Mary O'Kane wisely guides you through the power of the supportive dual role of the parent and child towards feeling safe and secure within themselves in our anxious world.

Allison Keating, Chartered Psychologist

This is an excellent guide for parents who are trying to support their children with anxiety, and a great tool for teachers to have in their classroom. It offers practical advice on how to create a safe and nurturing environment for your children to express their feelings. From dealing with phobias to separation anxiety this book covers it all. I particularly liked the step ladder approach - climbing a ladder and breaking tasks into small manageable pieces until you reach the goal. A tip I'll use in my own home too.

Mairéad Ronan, Broadcaster, Podcaster and Business owner

I devoured this book, could have read it in one sitting, I loved it. What an important book for the times we live in, a vital resource for any of us who have children in our lives (parents, guardians, grandparents, teachers, coaches). This book is up-to-the-minute relevant; it addresses how to help children around big life events, of which there have been plenty these past few years. If you're feeling at sea and unsure how to support your anxious child in this modern world, this book is for you. You'll come away with a new-found understanding of anxiety, as well as solid practical tips on how to help your child face their fears and find their brave.

Niamh Fitzpatrick, Psychologist

Anxious Children in an Anxious World

FACING FEARS AND FINDING BRAVE

Anxious Children in an Anxious World

Published 2023 by Dr Mary O'Kane
Copyright © Dr Mary O'Kane
ISBN: 978-1-916544-29-1

Publishing Information
Design & publishing services
provided by JM Agency

www.jm.agency
Kerry, Ireland

Anxious Children in an Anxious World

FACING FEARS AND FINDING BRAVE

DR MARY O'KANE

DISCLAIMER

This book is a general guide intended for information and educational purposes only. It should never be a substitute for the skill, knowledge, and experience of a qualified medical professional dealing with an individual case. While this book is intended as a general information resource, and all care has been taken in compiling its contents, each person and situation is unique. It is recommended that if a child or teenager is struggling with ongoing anxiety, the reader consult a qualified professional regarding the personal circumstances of that child.

DEDICATION

Sometimes our job is to protect our children from the rain,
To be the umbrella providing shelter.
But, more often, our job is to remind them,
That they are brave enough to withstand stormy weather.

Dr Mary O'Kane

This book is dedicated to Erin, Michael, and Kira
who have taught me so much about life, love, and myself.

Contents

Foreword

The challenge for any parenting advisor is to walk the delicate tightrope of empathy and practicality, of sympathy and science. Mary does it beautifully. Her advice, whether given in the pages of her books, one-to-one, or over the airwaves on shows like mine, always starts in the same place - genuine, heartfelt empathy for the child and parent. Whether it's a primary student with a school phobia, a teen with screen envy, a dad worrying about a distance growing between him and his kids, or a mum trying to interpret a world of conflict in a way her little ones can understand, Mary's starting position is always one of real concern for the person.

The great thing is that she then supports that with scientific insight, provided in practical accessible language. That approach is evident through the pages that follow here. Real life problems faced by every parent and family are answered with easily implementable solutions. And throughout Mary introduces us to some of the most interesting research and experiments in child and adolescent psychology, rooting actionable steps in academic insights.

And as you'll see as you read on, she writes with the same infectious positivity she brings to her clients and students; no problem is insurmountable, no challenge overwhelming - her fundamental position is that if you surround your children with love and listening then you can't go far wrong. But in between the love and the listening, if they throw the occasional tantrum, get a little overwhelmed by what they see on the news, fail the occasional test or shave the cat in protest because they didn't get that smartphone they wanted, then its handy to know what to do that will create the least conflict, provide the fastest results and leave the happiest family environment. And those answers follow…

– **Anton Savage, Broadcaster**

Introduction

When it comes to our children, knowledge is power. Psychology can teach us about how anxiety impacts the brain and the body. Research can teach us what interventions are proven to work and how we can use that knowledge. Others with similar experiences can share with us what has worked for them. I have spent many years, both professionally and personally, working to better understand anxiety and how best to support our children who struggle with it. My aim with this book is to create a resource that will break down lessons from psychology and research in a simple way, providing insight into the important role that adults play in helping children thrive in this anxious world. It is the book I wish I had read when my children were little.

Anxiety is felt on a spectrum. Although it is natural to feel some anxiety, for some children, it becomes something they struggle with. This book is aimed at parents, carers, and educators of children from preschool through to teenage years. It is for the adults in the lives of children for whom anxiety is impacting their ability to reach their full potential. These children need our love and support to help them find strategies to cope with their fears. It will also help adults in the lives of sensitive children who want to cultivate the resilience they need to thrive in this anxious world.

There are three very important things we can do as parents to support our children. Firstly, learn about anxiety, the links between the responses of our children's brains and the physiological impact on their bodies. Then share this information with our children. Anxiety is disempowering. Understanding what is happening in their brains and bodies helps our children regain some of that power. Secondly, we can equip them with self-regulation skills, which will help them to respond when anxiety kicks in. We can support them to develop these skills over time so that they can put them into practise when anxiety creeps into their lives. Thirdly, we can support them in finding the bravery we know they have within them. This involves navigating some challenging situations with our support. It involves coping with tricky emotions and learning to face their fears, baby-step by baby-step.

The goal is not to rid our children of anxiety completely. In fact, that is not possible. Instead, this book will introduce you to ways your child can learn to live with their fearful thoughts. We want them to find healthy ways to cope so that it does not become an overwhelming force in their lives. We don't want to pathologise anxiety. There is not something 'wrong' with our children who struggle in this way. It is a completely normal response to many situations. However, for some of our children, we need to help give them the strength to live bravely with the discomfort of their anxiety.

In all my years lecturing and working with parents, the most important thing I have learned is that children struggling with anxiety can learn to live with greater confidence. The support of 'one good adult' can be life-changing for a child. Having someone who understands the impact of anxiety on the brain and body and who is willing to work with them to find their inner courage, supporting them to approach the world with more confidence, makes all the difference. By gently pushing their limits, we are helping them to find the courage to face their fears. Every time they are brave and push through their anxiety, they build confidence in the world and strengthen the brain's connections that support this courageous behaviour. The time you spend doing this is worth every minute.

To do all the above, we also need to find the bravery we know that we have within ourselves. If you are anything like me, that can take a lot of deep breaths. But it can be done. I cannot give you a magic wand to wish your child's anxiety away, but the information in this book will provide you with the knowledge, understanding, and skills you need to support your child to push through their fears and flourish.

CHAPTER 1

Children's Social and Emotional Development

There is no such thing as a baby.
There is a baby and someone.

Donald Winnicott

From birth, babies are pre-programmed to seek interactions with their caregivers. These interactions impact their rapidly developing brains. Neurons, or nerve cells, in the brain are constantly making connections with each other as a response to social interaction. Each attempt at communication from the baby, cooing, smiling, or crying, is an opportunity for the parent to engage in what we call a 'serve and return' process. Like a game of tennis, the child interacts. Perhaps they make eye contact or snuggle into their carer, and the adult responds with a sound, a look, or a word. As the parent and child interact with each other, communicating with attention and responding to contact from each other, connections within the child's brain are strengthened. We know that responsive and attentive adult-child relationships build a strong foundation for learning and development.

Babies are also predisposed to engage in what we call 'meshing behaviours.' This is when the adult and child's behaviours fit in with each other during social interactions. We also know that mothers instinctively progressively allow their babies to be more active in these interactions. They slowly become a turn-taking collaboration between the pair. We see this often when a parent communicates with their baby using 'parentese,' a simple sing-song type of speech reserved for babies. The baby responds to mum by cooing and smiling. This, in turn, provokes another enthusiastic response from the mother. Baby responds again by gurgling and reaching out towards her mother, and the dance continues.

A famous experiment in psychology called the *Still Face Experiment* studied how babies crave human connection[1]. The experiment involved a mother facing her baby, holding a still face, meaning she showed no facial expression for a few minutes while the baby's reactions were observed. The babies make repeated attempts to engage with the mother. They wave their hands, vocalise to try to connect, and finally, become upset if they fail to gain a response. These babies immediately knew something was wrong with the mother's lack of response. The experiment is a reminder of the importance of reciprocal social exchanges between babies and their caregivers.

Examining the brain scans of babies brought up with responsive human connections shows that many different parts of their brains light up through nurturing parenting. Meanwhile, the scans of babies who have not benefited from these responsive relationships are different, with the amygdala (the area central to the fear response) most lit up, showing these children are more focused on survival than their more securely attached counterparts. This research reminds us why connection is important to our interactions with our children. Connection results in trust within a relationship.

It is so important for every parent to know that these everyday interactions between caregiver and child do not have to be perfect. Instead, we are looking for a 'good enough' fit between both partners to support the child through development and growth. We, as parents, take a bit of time to learn about the responses of our babies, and they are still learning to respond proactively. Both are engaged in the dance of learning how to connect.

These early relationships are crucial for children's brain development. They are the building blocks for strong future mental health, interpersonal skills, and academic performance. They lay the foundations for future development in terms of self-confidence and self-esteem, conflict resolution and self-regulation, and the capacity to go on and form stable relationships. We also know that newborn infants are born evolutionarily and psychologically prepared to initiate personal encounters. They do this in many ways.

Traditionally, research argued that the smiles of young babies were not 'real' but were what we call reflex smiles. The belief was that the baby was not feeling real emotion. Instead, the smile was an innate reflex. Indeed, many baby books still state that babies will not give a real 'social smile' until they are about eight weeks old. However, we now know that new-born babies have the capacity not only to imitate adult behaviour but also to respond in an interactive manner.

Learning From Psychology

Research also tells us that adults across the world use the same type of facial expressions when interacting with babies[2]. These include 'Special Happy' (an intense smile with open mouth) 'Fish Face' (puckered lips, a moderate smile and raised brows) and 'Mock Surprise' (raised brows, open mouth, often accompanied by an 'oooo' noise). Interestingly, recent research has found that these are the same expressions we use when interacting with our dogs!

Our role in these early relationships is even more important as we build on the child's interests to stimulate their learning journey. Children naturally reach out to us for connection, and we are pre-programmed to respond. This connection gives our children an insight into healthy relationships. It helps them understand other people's thoughts, feelings, and needs, helping them form cooperative relationships in the future. Studies on why young children laugh tell us that children's laughter is very much related to their interactions with others. They won't laugh at something vanishing from view on its own. They laugh when an adult makes the object disappear and reappear suddenly. Their laughter is primarily social. Once again, this brings us back to their connection with us and how that builds their emotional understanding and wellbeing.

 ## Learning From Psychology

Developmental Psychologist Jean Piaget told us that babies' laughter represents an important stage in development. If the child laughs, it means they are at the stage where they can understand a joke. They must understand the reason behind the humour, which gives us an insight into their emotional and cognitive development. Let's look at the game of Peekaboo, which is played across the world between parents and babies. The parent hides their eyes with their hands, then suddenly reveals them to squeals of delight from the baby. This is linked to Piaget's idea of *Object Permanence*, which is the idea that it takes babies time to understand that objects are still there when out of sight. Initially, the baby is completely surprised when Dad jumps out from behind the hands but slowly develops the expectation that he might be there behind them. So, she predicts that Dad will reappear again after he disappears until she gets to the point where she can enjoy the game of him hiding and reappearing again and again. This is the beginning of developing trust in the people and the world around her.

In these very individualised connections, we lay the foundations of future social and emotional development. It is our love, support, and connection with our children that are central to long-term wellbeing.

Early Brain Development

At birth, most of our formal brain structure has already developed. However, the internal workings of the brain continue to change and develop throughout childhood and adolescence. Years ago, psychologists used to believe that by the age of five to seven years, our children's brains were all but fully developed. We now know that this is not true. Their brains may be almost full-size, but development is ongoing. Developmental cognitive neuroscientists have now shown that our children's brains are still under development through to their mid-twenties. This comes as no surprise for those of us with teens and young adults!

Neurons are the information processing units of the brain responsible for receiving and transmitting information. Neurotransmitters carry signals from one neuron to another via synapses. This is a little bit like an electrical current running from one neuron to another. At birth, every neuron has an estimated 2,500 synapses, but by the age of three, this has grown to an estimated 15,000 synapses per neuron. Isn't that incredible? The connections we use more often become stronger and stronger, while the ones we use less often are considered less important, and these weaker connections are eliminated or pruned away. So, the functionality of our brain is constantly evolving and adapting to our changing environment. This is important to remember when considering our children's development, as it reminds us that their life experiences can re-shape their neural pathways.

Modern research has revealed that although the brain is more adaptable in childhood, it never fully loses the ability to change in response to learning. We call this skill plasticity. Up to approximately twelve years of age, the brain continues to make structural changes, adapting and modifying depending on individual circumstances and experiences. During the teenage years, a reorganisation of neurons and their synapses occurs. This pruning process starts towards the back of the brain, through the limbic system (often referred to as the emotional brain) and finishes with the most important part of the brain, the prefrontal cortex (often referred to as the thinking brain).

We used to speak about the nature-nurture debate in psychology, but now we usually refer to interactionism. There is a dynamic relationship between our genes and our environment. Mental health issues, such as anxiety, are often a combination of a genetic predisposition and the impact of environmental factors. It is the combination of brain development and the context in which a child is developing that is important in the early years and, indeed, throughout the lifespan. The impact of our relationships with our children is not more important at any one stage of development. Instead, the nature of these relationships varies by age and developmental stage.

The Importance of Attachment

We know the early years are vitally important and that, from birth, babies connect with those around them. But *how* do these interactions impact on their development?

Warm, loving relationships provide comfort and are how babies develop a sense of their worth. As caregivers respond to infants' cries, facial expressions, and gestures, the first lines of communication are opened. When the baby realises their needs will be met, it helps them to develop trust. It is no surprise that when speaking about infants, we stress the importance of these secure relationships.

The concept of secure attachment was developed by British psychologist John Bowlby, who referred to attachments as important for young children's healthy mental development[3]. If a child is frightened, she will seek comfort and care from her primary caregiver. This makes sense in terms of survival, as children who maintain proximity to their primary carer are more likely to survive into adulthood. This relationship teaches children they can depend on their needs to be consistently met, which is the foundation for secure attachment.

Based on these interactions, the child develops an internal working model or a personal theory of how the world works. As this relationship provides the support the child needs, they will seek it out at times of fear. They use it as a secure base from which they can explore the world. Bowlby's work led to the argument that children who grow up to demonstrate independence and self-reliance have parents who are supportive when needed but who also encourage independence and autonomy.

From the Horse's Mouth

Do you remember when your child was little, and she dropped something from her highchair only to have you pick it up for her and return it? Oh, the joy and excitement, particularly if it was your first child. I remember this happening so well with my eldest. If you were anything like me, you probably called your partner to witness this wonderful event. Although, it might not have seemed quite so exciting ninety-nine times later! But when I think of my daughter dropping things from her highchair only to have me pick them up and return them, I realise this was how she gradually learned to take a risk and let something go, safe in the knowledge that it would return.

It seems that we intuitively provide a holding relationship for the infant. We use empathy to provide a reliable environment responsive to the needs of the child. We often see parents do this by mirroring the baby's responses, responding to the baby's expressions, and reflecting their love back in their responses. Connection with us gives our children the self-belief to take flight.

A Word to the Wise

Toni Morrison, author of *The Bluest Eye*, has spoken about the messages we give our children as we interact with them. She asks when our children walk into the room, does our face light up? She says we often look at our children and check for little things, such as whether they have brushed their hair or pulled their socks up. But when we do this, our faces register disapproval. We think we are showing love by caring for them, but they see faces watching them with a critical eye. Instead, she argues, we need to make sure our faces light up when we see our children. We want them to receive the message that our hearts are glad to see them when they walk into a room.

Attachment theory tells us that as our children grow and develop, they should form strong attachments with their primary carers. But, over time, children should loosen their attachments to parents, as they need them less. As they become stronger and more capable, they naturally move away from the secure base of their family and venture out on their own. But children who struggle with anxiety sometimes don't realise how strong and brave they are. They continue sending distress signals to us for support because they haven't learned that they can do hard things. When our anxious child sends out these distress cues to us, what do we do? We respond and rescue. Instead, we want them to know that they can do so much for themselves. Throughout this book, we will return to our role in helping our children find their inner strength.

Temperament and Goodness of Fit

Temperament describes the way the infant interacts with the world. When considering an infant's temperament, researchers look at areas such as levels of activity, adaptability to new situations, intensity of interactions, sensitivity to the environment, and distractibility. Most parents of more than one child, and indeed most educators, will tell you that even children from the same families can show very different personalities. We know from research into children's dispositions that babies come into this world with different temperament types.

One of the most influential studies examining temperament conducted by Thomas and Chess was called the New York Longitudinal Study. It lasted for decades and identified nine temperamental traits.

- Activity – the level and extent of motor activity.
- Regularity – the rhythmicity of functions such as sleep and wakefulness.
- Initial Reaction – response to new people and situations.
- Adaptability – flexibility at points of change.
- Sensitivity – sensory sensitivity to stimuli.
- Intensity – energy levels or intensity of reactions.
- Mood – general mood or disposition.
- Distractibility – distractibility from what they are doing.
- Attention Span – attention and perseverance with activities.

Looking at these traits, they developed three temperament styles:

Easy Temperament: These children tend to be easily adaptable, calm, and not too easily upset. They cope well with both routine and change.

Difficult Temperament: These children do not adapt as easily to routines. They are more intense in their reactions and more fearful of new people and situations.

Slow to Warm Up Temperament: These children tend to be cautious of new people and experiences. However, they will adapt over time and at their own pace.

From the Horse's Mouth

I should say, at this point, that I struggle with labelling any child as 'difficult.' Even if, from a parenting perspective, we might feel they are more challenging to parent than our other children. I prefer to think of these children as highly sensitive. They may seem quite emotionally reactive, but remember, these children are often deep thinkers, highly empathetic, and heart-centred. Our world could certainly do with more of those traits.

Although many children do not fall neatly into one category, temperament can help us understand our children's strengths and the areas in which we may need to support them.

Closely linked to temperament is personality. Psychologists have identified the 'Big Five' personality dimensions linked to enduring individual differences in behaviour. Although these have been identified through research with adults, there is evidence that they apply to childhood and adolescence and that personality can be described as a set of variations across these five aspects. They are:

- **Extroversion**: the extent to which a person actively engages with their world. People who are high in this personality trait are usually outgoing, talkative, enthusiastic, and confident. Those low in this trait are more likely to prefer solitude and dislike being the centre of attention.

- **Conscientiousness**: the ability to control impulses. This is reflected in reliable, responsible behaviour. Those who are low in this trait are more likely to dislike structure, schedules, and deadlines.
- **Agreeableness**: this relates to compassion, warmth, and sensitivity. This is seen as affection, kindness, and trust in others. Those low in this dimension tend to be more competitive and combative.
- **Openness to experience**: this reflects levels of curiosity and imagination. People who are high in this trait can be described as original, curious, or having artistic tendencies. Those who are low in this trait are more likely to resist change or new ideas.
- **Neuroticism**: this is reflected in the extent to which we find the world distressing or threatening. Those high on this trait are more likely to worry and be anxious. Those low on this dimension are more stable emotionally.

These five primary personality traits represent a range between two extremes (for example, extraversion vs introversion) and each of us lies somewhere in the spectrum between these extremes for each dimension. Individual personalities feature each of these traits to some extent. We can also differ on the more specific facets within each trait, for example, being high in originality and curiosity but less artistic. There is evidence, however, that test scores on these five dimensions are stable over time, from childhood to adulthood. We also know that temperament and personality impact not only our worldview but also our interactions with others and how they respond to us, which can impact our mental health and wellbeing.

For that reason, when we consider temperament, it is also important to consider the concept of *Goodness of Fit*. This idea is that the match between child and caregiver is more important than temperament alone. If the environment in which the child is developing, including the people in that environment, suits the child's temperament and is a good fit, then parenting can be easier. If parent and child temperaments are less of a good fit, the parent will find their role more challenging and may have to adapt to meet the needs of the individual child. This idea reminds us of the importance of using approaches that fit our child's temperament. When we feel challenged by a child's behaviour, we can remember that they are just responding to the world in a way their temperament will allow. This can help us adapt to their individual needs.

Australian author and educator Maggie Dent describes children's temperament on a scale from 'lamb' to 'rooster.' She advises that lambs are quieter children. They are accommodating and often seem quite content with life. These children are sensitive to discipline, can become distressed easily, and can be shy. However, they are also easy-going, patient, and thrive on routine. These children often have a well-developed sense of social justice and have a natural degree of empathy from a young age. Roosters are on the opposite end of the scale. They are often strong-willed, loud, and bursting with energy. These children are more likely to be highly independent, stubborn, and argumentative but can be fast learners, entertaining, and adventurous. They love opportunities to let off steam, whether in outdoor pursuits or hobbies such as dancing or sports.

If we consider this analogy, neither the lamb nor the rooster is 'better' than the other. They have different strengths and challenges. And remember, these are two ends of a scale. Few children are at the far end of each end. Most are a blend of lamb and rooster qualities. However, we can use these 'types' to guide the competencies we might focus on to support our children best. If we consider our lambs, to support these children best, we need to build their confidence, build assertiveness skills, and encourage safe risk-taking. However, for our roosters, we can encourage their independence by giving them autonomy by encouraging their adventurous spirit while also supporting them to develop empathy and kindness.

So, we know that both interactions with others and goodness of fit are important to consider when supporting our children. Our children absorb information from observing our behaviours and interactions with us, which brings us to consider the very important role of the adult in children's development.

One Good Adult

All the above reminds us that we should never underestimate the part we play in supporting our children to thrive in this world. By providing a secure base on which the child can rely, we give them the confidence to go out into the world and try new experiences. Doing this is easier for the child with the knowledge that we are there in the background for support if needed. Knowing they have a 'safe haven' which they can return to for reassurance or guidance, gives them the security to explore.

Research reminds us again and again of the importance of having *one good adult* in the life of a child. This acts as a buffer against stress and leads to more positive mental health. Having this support plays an important part in helping a child or young person deal with life's challenges rather than crumbling under pressure. Seeking support from others when encountering difficulties and using this support at times of stress is an active coping strategy. These strategies are key to navigating life's difficulties, as compared to avoidant coping strategies. It appears that the support of a trusted adult helps our children to take a more active approach to challenges, using this safe, supportive relationship to enable them to problem-solve when issues arise.

NES Scotland has worked with children and teens to develop a 'job description' for this one good adult. The criteria for the role include:

- A kind, approachable, and respectful manner.
- Being open-minded, fair, and trustworthy.
- Accepting children for who they are.
- Actively listening to children.
- Taking worries and concerns seriously.

- Helping find solutions to problems.
- Challenging children to push their boundaries.
- Just being there.

In summary, one good adult should be supportive, a good listener, empathetic, and non-judgemental. Every child deserves to have someone who believes in them. Even when they may not believe in themselves, an adult they know is always in their corner. But when looking at the role of one good adult, we also need to put this in perspective. The wording is one 'good' adult, not one 'perfect' adult for a reason. Our children do not need us to be perfect. They need someone who believes in them and wants the best for them. Indeed, the research findings mentioned above, using the still-face situation, report that mother-infant interactions are in a mismatched state up to 70% of the time. This reminds us that we do not have to be perfect parents – in fact, no such thing exists – getting it right 30% of the time is perfectly imperfect!

Having said that, as the parent of a child who has struggled with anxiety, I know we can be very hard on ourselves when we get it wrong. We know that building meaningful relationships with our children is central to positive emotional development. However, remember you are only human, and there will be days that you say or do the wrong thing. The idea of 'rupture and repair' is the one thing I always return to when I feel I have messed up. This term describes the cycle of little moments of disconnection (the rupture), which then lead back to reconnection with our children (the repair). The good news is that in a healthy relationship, we are usually in harmony with our child approximately a third of the time. For another third, we are often in a state of rupture, and for the final third, we are (hopefully) in a state of repair. The ruptures can range from minor misunderstandings to bigger arguments. But repair is what is truly important. After making a mistake, I always try to come back and repair. This means apologising for my actions, owning the error without making excuses, and letting my child know I will try to do better. Then, I try my best not to beat myself up about it. I remind myself that it is in moments of repair that trust is built in relationships. Trust and resilience are built because we've come through this shift from disconnection to reconnection. Paediatrician and psychoanalyst Donald Winnicott developed the concept of good enough mothering[4]. We now use the term, *good enough parent*, in recognition that the role of the parent, or primary caregiver, does not always reside with the mother. Winnicott starts by reminding us that babies are psychologically fragile, so their caregivers should be highly attuned to their needs in the first few months of life. But he argues we should naturally move from an initial feeling of devotion to the child to an understanding that we cannot meet their every need. This is important as the child needs to experience minor frustrations within their world. He believed this benefited their development and reasoned that children need to experience small disappointments to better equip themselves to face life's challenges. As the child experiences these minor blips, they learn to tolerate some frustration. He argues that none of us could sustain being perfect long term. We cannot give our child our undivided attention 24 hours a day, every day.

From the Horse's Mouth

I remember driving on a motorway with my youngest sitting in her car seat in the back of the car. She dropped her soother out of reach and called for me to get it. But as I was driving, I couldn't help her out. I remember the shocked look on her face – this person who was supposed to meet her every need had failed. This was not going as planned in her mind. She made her displeasure very clear to me, but what did she learn from this minor blip? She learned that the person she had thought was at her beck and call was not, in fact, perfect. Her mum was not Superwoman. But she also learned that it wasn't the end of the world. She learned that she could cope when things went wrong. Moments like this teach our children that in life, they will face challenges, but they are strong and capable enough to survive them, even when we cannot be on hand to support them. The point is that these minor blips benefit our children as they need us to occasionally let them down so they can learn to survive and thrive in an imperfect world.

The important point to remember is that to be the best parent we can be means being human. While we should be caring and empathetic, we do not have to be faultless. Our flaws are necessary for independent development to take place.

So, what is a good enough parent? Good enough parents know they will make mistakes but strive to do their best. Good enough parents know their children will make mistakes, but this is part of the learning process. Good enough parents try to understand their children's needs and their perspectives. Good enough parents know that the core of what we do is to create a strong and lasting connection that will carry us through the tough times.

One recent research study on teens and young adults confirmed this for us. The 2019 *My World 2 Survey* on mental health involved more than 19,000 twelve to twenty-five-year-olds[5]. This research reinforced the importance of the presence of a consistently supportive adult figure. This was noted as one of the most important factors in times of distress. These teens and young adults reminded us of the important role we play when they are struggling. In the words of Sinead, one of the respondents in the study: '*If I'm in trouble in my life, I don't need to be rescued or airlifted out of whatever crisis I'm in. I need someone to engage with me and help me grow through whatever I need to face.*' The teens in the study who reported that they had one good adult in their lives were more connected to others, more confident, and were better able to cope with difficulties than those without the presence of adult support.

For those of us with a child who struggles with anxiety, the one good adult concept is important to remember. We do not have to be perfect. We do not need to have all the answers. Instead, our children need to know that we are standing with them, learning about anxiety and how best to guide them and advocate for them. As Sinead reminds us so eloquently above, our role as one good adult is not to rescue. Instead, it is to support our children in growing and developing the skills to cope with the anxiety they are facing. One of the important ways we can do this is to increase our knowledge and understanding of what is happening to our children in the spiral of anxiety.

CHAPTER 2

Anxious Children: Brains and Bodies

When the pressures of modern life
meet the ancient circuitry of our brains, anxiety happens.
I call this 'the perfect storm' except there is nothing
perfect about it.

Dr Malie Coyne[6]

The Cambridge dictionary defines anxiety as *an uncomfortable feeling of nervousness or worry about something that is happening or might happen in the future.* It is a feeling of apprehension that develops when we anticipate a threatening situation, whether that situation is real or imagined. When talking about anxiety in children, psychologists often describe it as an over-estimation of the danger involved in a situation and an under-estimation of their ability to cope. The issue is that children can get into a cycle of anxiety, leading to more anxiety, meaning they can become over-sensitive to the stresses of life.

However, anxiety is not something we want to eradicate completely. Now, this might sound completely counterintuitive, but anxiety is part of our body's internal protection mechanism, our inner alarm, which helps us to survive danger. It is perfectly normal. In fact, moderate levels of anxiety can be productive, helping us to stay alert and motivated to achieve. Every child will experience anxiety from time to time. For example, when starting a new school year, when performing in the Christmas play, or before a school test.

If we think about our own experiences of childhood, it can remind us that every child worries. Childhood is a time of firsts, a time of new experiences and challenges. From our experience of starting preschool to our first day of school to our first school tour. From our first time riding a bike or our first swimming lesson to our first sleepover at a friend's house. As we grow into teens, our first crush, our first date, our first kiss. These are all exciting moments but can often be times of worry, too. Even as adults, we all feel anxious at times. Taking our driving test, our first job interview, or giving the best man speech. The list goes on and on. What does this tell us? That anxiety is a perfectly normal emotion.

It is also important to know that certain fears or anxieties are common at various stages of childhood. Psychology tells us that across cultures, children experience similar fears at predictable stages of development. These anxieties follow a general progression linked to cognitive development – your child's ability to make sense of the world. Below are some of the common fears you can expect at approximate stages of development:

- Infants and Toddlers - strangers; separation; loud noises.
- Preschoolers - costumed characters; sleeping alone; separation.
- Early School Age - storms; getting lost; scary TV characters.
- Middle School Age - finding friends; bullying; academic performance; athletic performance.
- Adolescence - judgement by peers; rejection from potential romantic partners; bodily changes; eco-anxiety; world issues.

These fears and worries are a normal part of childhood, and many children experience them. However, for some children, anxiety can become an issue. These children are more hypervigilant than others. They are on high alert to a greater extent. We usually say that a child's anxiety is becoming unhealthy when the demands it places on the child outweigh the resources and inner reserves they have, such as resilience, self-belief and coping skills. If anxiety starts to flood our children's systems, then it becomes problematic. Looking at the statistics below, we can see that anxiety is becoming more challenging for children worldwide.

 ## Learning From Psychology

Research from the University of Pennsylvania[7] reports that levels of anxiety in children in first-world countries have risen from 11% in 2012 to 20.5% in 2021. These figures are taken from a meta-analysis of twenty-nine studies worldwide.

In the UK in 2021, the NHS reported that one in six children in England had experienced a mental health difficulty[8]. In 2022, the Good Childhood Report[9] advised that five children in every classroom in England are likely to have a mental health problem. Looking at the teenage group alone, the NHS reported in 2022 that one in four teens aged 17-19 have a mental health difficulty, an increase from one in six in 2021.

A recent Australian study[10] reported that the rate of anxiety in 16–24-year-olds is 21% for boys and 41% for girls, having risen from 15% in 2007. This study also reported that the number of Australian teens experiencing clinical levels of anxiety has doubled in the past 15 years.

In Ireland, it is reported that by the age of thirteen, 1 in 3 children will have experienced some form of mental health difficulty. In terms of the most common issues, anxiety is high on the list[11]. By the age of 24, this rose to 1 in 2 young adults struggling with their mental health.

I do not present you with the statistics above to frighten you. Instead, I want you to recognise that your child is not alone. From a positive perspective, much of the research has confirmed what we know about *one good adult* and has found that the presence of a consistently supportive adult figure is one of the most crucial factors at times of distress. Interestingly, children in these research studies often report that they were most happy with their family, a reminder of the importance of family connection to wellbeing.

However, considering the statistics presented above, the importance of our children understanding what is taking place when they feel anxious and learning about ways to help calm and manage their wellbeing is clear. For those of us with a child who struggles with anxiety, the findings that the support of family and *one good adult* is important to remember. As we increase our knowledge and understanding of what is happening to our children in the spiral of anxiety, it leaves us in a stronger place to support them.

From The Horse's Mouth

Very often, children believe they are the only ones experiencing anxiety, and it is important they know that they are not alone. When giving talks to teens, I try to remind them of this. As they look around their classroom, they find it hard to believe that the 'cool kids' might struggle with anxiety, too - the girl who is the brightest in the class, the boy who is captain of the football team, the child who always takes the starring role in the school play. I remember being at a *One Direction* concert with one of my children, looking around at the excitement of the young fans. Would they ever believe that Zayn Malik struggles with anxiety? Would children watching Emma Stone play the part of Cruella believe that she struggled with panic attacks for years of her childhood? Do young tennis fans watching Naomi Osaka compete know that she had to withdraw from Wimbledon, citing mental health reasons? It is important that our children realise they are not alone in experiencing anxiety. We can normalise anxiety when we speak to them about people they respect and admire who have also struggled with anxiety in their lives but who have also gone on to achieve remarkable things. This can make them aware that anxiety is something others experience and overcome to live happy, successful lives.

The term *psychoeducation* refers to the process of teaching people about their mental health, specifically focusing on areas in which they are struggling. This is a particularly important intervention to start with when trying to support a child struggling with anxiety. Anxiety can start to control their lives and leave them feeling powerless. Taking the time to fully explain the causes of anxiety and the symptoms they are living with is the first step in claiming back their power. Understanding how anxiety works in their brain and their body will help them not only feel more in control of their situation but is the first step in understanding how the various treatment methods to help them cope with anxious episodes work. As you normalise anxiety with your child and talk to them about the struggles of others, remind them that anxiety is something they can overcome. They can learn to live with greater confidence in their world and in themselves.

The Impact of Anxiety

Anxiety impacts our children's lives in numerous ways. Children who struggle with anxiety might be fearful of making mistakes or of making a fool of themselves in public. They might avoid sports or performance-related activities where they feel they will be on show. They are often overly aware of the judgements of others. They can struggle to fall asleep at night as they lie in bed, ruminating over the day's events. Although we all reflect to some extent, these children tend to go around in circles, which can become problematic. Some will have difficulty sleeping alone. They may wake in the middle of the night and want to sneak into their parent's bed. Anxiety can also result in problems going to school, with the child citing sick tummy, headaches and so on.

No matter the intensity or duration of their anxiety, we know that ongoing anxiety is disempowering for our children. One thing that can help them claw back their power is understanding what is happening within their bodies. So, it is important to explain anxiety to your child in an age-appropriate way.

The Science Behind Anxiety

If we are to start to explain anxiety to our children, the first thing to explain is that anxiety is a good thing. This sounds completely counterintuitive because anxiety can feel awful.

How does anxiety feel for your child? There are many physical symptoms of anxiety your child may experience. Often, they feel their heart racing, then a feeling of breathlessness or short, shallow breathing. This can result in the child feeling lightheaded or dizzy. They can also feel weak or experience shaking hands and legs. Some may experience excessive sweating, feeling hot and flushed, and a dry mouth. Others may suffer from stomach pains, a feeling like they might throw up, and may experience frequent urination or diarrhoea. While sleeping, they may undergo very restless nights, with teeth grinding and jaw clenching quite common among children struggling with anxiety. These symptoms can be both physically and emotionally draining.

It can help our children to know that anxiety stems from a system designed to protect them. That knowledge alone can help a child to feel more empowered. Anxiety is a system handed down by evolution to keep us safe. This leads us to consider two parts of our brain: the thinking brain and the emotional brain. Let's start with the emotional brain, the limbic system, which helps us deal with our emotions and memories.

• The Amygdala aka The Toddler

The *Amygdala* is a particularly important part of the emotional brain. The amygdala takes in information from our senses and helps to protect us from any threats in our environment. It reacts quickly when it senses danger and is like a little internal warrior trying to protect us.

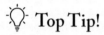 **Top Tip!**

I suggest that younger children imagine the amygdala as a little toddler trying to protect them. Imagine him in the centre of the brain, sitting on guard, ready to respond to any danger. If they have younger siblings who are toddlers, they will know that toddlers don't react calmly to danger.

When the amygdala receives information from our senses that could mean danger, it instantly starts a reaction inside our bodies to protect us. We call this the fight or flight response. The amygdala thinks something might hurt you, so it springs into action to protect you. This response has helped humans to survive since hunter-gatherer times.

Imagine you are living back in hunter-gatherer times. You are out hunting and hear a rustle in the bushes behind you. Before you can even turn your head to see if there is danger lurking, your amygdala will have responded. It sends signals to release stress hormones such as adrenaline and cortisol, which cause physical reactions inside your body. Your heart pounds, beating faster as blood rushes to your extremities - your arms and hands in case you need to fight, and your legs and feet in case you need to run. Your breathing changes, becoming faster, making you breathless, and you may feel flushed or dizzy. The amygdala sees no need to digest food, as it wants to save energy to fight or flee, so it slows down the digestive system. These responses are all designed to help protect you. The amygdala is preparing you in case you need to either fight a tiger lurking in those bushes or run away from it.

This system helps us to respond to the many challenges we face. But if this response is invoked by everyday life events, then the trouble starts. For our children, the amygdala might respond this way to seeing their friends standing away from them in the schoolyard, whispering to each other. It could respond this way if they do something they think is embarrassing and other students in the class laugh. For older children, it could respond this way if they put a photo up on Instagram that gets very few likes. Their worrying thoughts bring about the same response as a tiger in the bushes did for our ancestors. The problem is that the amygdala has lightning-fast reflexes. It moves to protect us without sending messages to the second part of our brain – the thinking brain. This area of the brain considers the level of risk and how to respond.

The takeaway here is that the amygdala is very important as it protects us from danger. In an emergency, we need our body to activate an emergency response in milliseconds. Not doing so could be the difference between life and death. Before we consciously consider the danger, the body has detected a threat and activated this response mechanism. This response is very powerful and exceptionally fast, rather than being accurate. In some of our children, the amygdala can seem a little overly vigilant.

Learning From Psychology

Research from Stanford University School of Medicine[12] examined the size and connectivity of the amygdala in children and found that it could predict levels of anxiety. They found that a larger amygdala and the stronger its connections with other brain regions responsible for attention, vigilance, and regulation of emotion were a predictor for greater levels of anxiety. Similar findings were noted in studies of adults with anxiety disorders, which also found that their amygdalae were more likely to be larger and more highly connected. The authors noted that they were surprised the size and connectivity differences were so significant due to the young age of the children (7-9 years) but also that their anxiety levels were still too low to be considered clinical, yet these differences were clearly apparent.

• The Prefrontal Cortex, aka the Teacher

While the amygdala responds to save our lives, another part of our brain considers whether this response is needed in this individual situation. The part of the brain responsible for this type of thinking is called the *Prefrontal Cortex*. It is at the front of our brain, behind our forehead. This is the part of the brain responsible for higher-level thinking – things like organisation, planning, decision making and reasoning. It is the centre of rational, logical thought. This area of the brain helps us work things out. But, when we are angry, stressed, or anxious, the amygdala stops information from getting to it.

 Top Tip!

If your child imagines the amygdala as a little toddler sitting in the centre of the brain, ready for action, then they could imagine the prefrontal cortex as a little teacher, prepared to approach a situation with logic.

When a difficult situation arises, the little toddler can take control, and this thinking part of the brain - the little teacher - is turned offline. We are relying on action rather than thought to deal with the situation. Why would the amygdala think sending the prefrontal cortex offline at a time of danger is a good idea? Because your brain just wants you to be safe. It doesn't want you to take the time necessary to weigh up the danger or to process an event. Instead, it wants you to respond in milliseconds. As adults, our prefrontal cortex is better developed, which is why we find it easier to reach it at times of stress. But if you can think back to a time when you were anxious, you may well remember not being able to reach this thinking brain either.

From the Horse's Mouth

There are occasions in the past when I have been up at a height (for example, on a cliff walk) with my children. I find heights terrifying. I have become overwhelmed by anxiety and seemed to lose all sense of reason. My brain was racing, my heart was pounding, and I could feel the anxiety pulsing through my body. Even though my thinking brain should have been aware that my children were safely away from the cliff's edge, all rational thought had departed. All I could feel was fear. I have often found that when my child's anxiety seems senseless to me, it can help me to remember how I feel when I am exposed to heights. My fear might not seem logical to someone else, but to me, it is very real.

This response from the amygdala worked perfectly back in hunter-gatherer times when we were out dealing with physically risky situations every day. But it is as if our brains have not caught up in evolutionary terms with our modern world and the challenges it brings us. This very quick response, firing on all cylinders when we no longer have a physical challenge to respond to, is not always helpful. It can leave us dealing with the fight or flight response and the awful physical feelings which come with it. These feelings can make us even more anxious, but our logical thinking brain has been cut out of the loop, so it cannot help us evaluate the danger in a logical way. This little toddler is trying to protect you, but if you don't need protection, you need to help it reset. When we are calm, the amygdala is calm, and information flows to the prefrontal cortex so we can make better decisions.

• The Smoke Alarm

This brings us to another important aspect to understand about the amygdala. It can't tell the difference between real danger and perceived danger. It can be helpful to remind our children of this fact.

To understand this better, we can compare the amygdala to a smoke alarm. If we think about the smoke alarms in our homes, they cannot tell the difference between the house burning down and burnt toast. They don't assess the level of risk. The only goal is to warn you of danger.

The smoke alarm analogy can be useful to describe how children respond to anxiety. Imagine your smoke alarm goes off in your kitchen. Your child (who doesn't struggle with anxiety) hears the alarm from the other room. She may wait for a while to see if the alarm continues before responding. If it does, she will come running into the kitchen to see what's happening. She will assess the situation and perhaps realise you have just burned some toast. She is reassured there is no real risk of fire and grabs a tea towel, flapping it in the air to re-set the alarm. This is how most of us respond to anxiety. We respond to our internal alarm, evaluate the situation, assess the level of risk, and once we recognise that the perceived danger is manageable, we reset our alarm.

However, for some children, it is as if their alarm is set a little too sensitively. Now, imagine your child who struggles with anxiety hears your smoke alarm. She won't delay. She will respond on alert at the very first sound. She will run into the kitchen and see the toast smouldering in the toaster. She might start to feel some reassurance, but then it is as if she has difficulty evaluating the level of risk. She thinks, 'Hold on, that toast is still smouldering. It could go on fire at any moment. I'm not sure we are safe.' This time, the child's assessment of the problem is not quite as accurate as the previous example. She might get a tea towel and flap it in the air to reset the alarm, but she is only half-heartedly flapping as she is still convinced there could be danger. It is as if her whole system is a little off-kilter. Her initial response to the alarm, her evaluation of the situation, and her final reaction are all heightened. This is what it is like for our children who struggle with anxiety.

Give it a Try!

After a period of anxiety when things have resolved (never during), it can also be useful for our children to use this distinction to consider how anxious they have been about a perceived threat. For example, say your child has been worried all week about going to a birthday party on Saturday. Maybe the birthday boy is not in his close friendship group, and his best friend isn't invited. All week, he worries about whether he should go. Will he know anyone there? Will he be OK mixing with this unknown group of children? You persuade him to be brave, to give it a try. He goes, and he ends up enjoying himself. The following day, you might ask him this question about his previous anxiety, 'Was the house burning down, or was it just burnt toast?' It can help children see that the events they were so worried about were not so important in the bigger scheme of things. Their amygdala had overestimated the level of threat.

• The Hippocampus, aka The Helpful Hippo

If you explain this system to children, they will often ask, why me? Why, when my brother is so laid back, he is almost horizontal, and my sister never seems to worry about much, do I feel so anxious? If we all have the same system in our brains, why am I struggling this way? This brings us to another important part of this system - the *Hippocampus*. The role of the hippocampus is to process information and organise and retrieve memories.

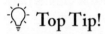 Top Tip!

I suggest young children imagine the Hippocampus to be a little helpful hippopotamus. Imagine her sitting beside the little amygdala with a notepad in front of her. When the little toddler responds to danger and starts to panic, it is as if she makes a note of that situation, 'Oh, that looks dangerous, we must remember that' or 'I didn't like the look of that situation. Make a note to be more careful next time.' She is storing away our memories and making sure we can retrieve useful information later.

But this is, in fact, making us more fearful. The children whose amygdala seems a little more sensitive have these messages reinforced by the hippocampus.

Think about the experience of going on a rollercoaster. Say a child loves the experience. They scream with excitement on the ride and wave their hands in the air. It is not that their amygdala doesn't register danger. It is as if their amygdala registers the danger as thrilling, exciting, and exhilarating. They come off the ride to their dad waiting for them. They might run right past him, shouting that they are going to queue up again for another ride. Their experience and memories of the ride are fantastic.

Now, let's take another child who is terrified by the experience. He comes off the ride and meets his dad waiting for him. He tells Dad it was the most terrifying experience he has ever had. His belt was loose and could have come off at any time. He could have been flung from the ride. The car nearly shot off the ride as it reached the top of the hill, and he was sure the noise he heard was the sound of the bolts loosening. He insists he is never going on the rollercoaster again. Imagine his dad persuades him to try the bumper cars instead. The child might consider giving it a try but could transfer his bad experience to the less scary ride. When the safety bar comes down, he thinks of the roller coaster. When the bumper car starts, the noise reminds him of the bolts. His brain registers the similarities between the two rides, and he struggles with the idea of feeling safe on either of them. It is as if a negative loop occurs as the hippocampus stores negative memories of being anxious, and then the amygdala becomes more anxious about this and similar experiences.

These two children have gone through the same ride but have experienced it very differently. That rollercoaster could be your home, a classroom, a football team, or any individual context. The setting is the same for all children, but their responses to and experiences within the environment can be very different.

• The Neural Pathways, aka The River

We know our children's brains are flexible, which means they can change and adapt. Functional changes in our brains occur when we learn new things and take in new information. This is what we call *neuroplasticity*, which is probably one of the most important findings ever made in neuroscience. It means that our brains are not fixed. They can develop and grow. We also know that the connections in our brains which are used more often become more embedded. The human brain is made up of an estimated one hundred billion neurons, making a total of one hundred trillion neural connections. When our brain cells communicate frequently, the connections between them strengthen. The pathways in the brain that are used again and again begin to transmit faster and faster, and stronger neural pathways are formed.

If we imagine these pathways working in a similar way to a river developing, it starts with little tributaries high in the mountains. As they grow, they join and become a trickling stream. These small streams meet and grow larger until they become a strong river. This is similar to how the pathways in the brain become stronger and more embedded. But also, the neural pathways which are not used are eventually reduced. If we think of the river and prune back these little tributaries by blocking them with dams, they start to run dry. As we dry up the watercourse, the riverbed will become smaller, and the edges will eventually become overgrown with plants again. If we support our children to cope with danger, face their fears, and ride the wave of their anxiety, we help the neural pathways in their brains adapt and change.

We know from psychology that neuroplasticity follows generalised rules. Some of these are important to note, as they relate to the advice in later chapters as we discuss how we can support our children. The first is Hebb's rule: *'Neurons that Fire Together, Wire Together'*. In other words, if pathways in the brain are being used regularly, they become strengthened. The brain relies on repetitive stimulation to build stronger connections. Equally, if pathways in the brain are not being used, the brain begins to sideline them. These unused pathways become weaker and weaker over time. This is often summed up as *'Use It or Lose It'*. These rules remind us that the support we put in place to help our children self-regulate when they feel anxious and help them face their fears can cause changes in their brain development.

Fight, Flight, Freeze, and Fawn

When the brain's limbic system responds to stress or trauma, we often refer to the process as the '*fight or flight*' response. This is shorthand for the fight, flight, freeze, and fawn stress response. These responses have developed over millions of years of evolution. When triggered, we all have different stress responses. These are our primitive survival responses kicking in, and we tend to fall into one or more of these four areas.

The way an individual child responds stems from their individual instincts and their learned responses. In different situations, different responses may be more relevant. But our children can sometimes learn to rely too much on one of these responses. Let's consider what fight, flight, freeze, and fawn look like in our children.

The fight response is the most obvious to onlookers. Fight feels reactive. It could be a child who seems explosive. We see very open, angry responses. Parents might say their child seems constantly defiant. The child externalises their anxiety. They may try to control the situation, be argumentative, and demanding. Sometimes, these children are labelled as 'bold' (I take issue with this label. Often, this is a child who is overwhelmed by the expectations placed on them, a child who does not have the capability to deal with the situation they find themselves in). Sometimes, they may lash out or shout out to protect themselves. They are children who display 'big' emotions. When a child has a triggered fight response, the most important thing we can do as parents is to create an environment for regulation. The most effective way to do this is to look at ourselves. We need to be a calm presence. First comes silence, followed by empathy to validate their feelings.

Remember, although fight might seem unhealthy, it makes perfect sense to react aggressively to a threat in some situations. In past times, and indeed in some situations of conflict, this was a very natural response if threatened by a predator.

 **Top Tip!**

For a child who automatically goes into the fight response, a very physical activity such as jumping on a trampoline, shaking out the stress, doing jumping jacks, running, or dancing can be a very effective response to help self-regulate.

Flight feels more like a need to escape and get away. The aim here is to try to escape the threat. It is another very common response, although it may be less obvious than fight. The child will do anything to remove themselves from the source of the anxiety. They may isolate themselves from others and withdraw into themselves. This can be seen in a child who tends to feel trapped in challenging situations and is very much about conflict avoidance. Parents may say that their child is an over-thinker.

This response can be physically displayed in jumpiness, restlessness, or jittery movements. Children in flight mode are often hypervigilant and may have difficulty resting and sleeping. As mentioned above, show empathy and validation, and then you can suggest coping strategies to help ground the child. A weighted toy or weighted blanket can help the child feel more secure.

 Learning From Psychology

Research by Harvard University studied the impact of taking a 'power pose' on cortisol levels[13]. In the study, test subjects had to spend two minutes sitting in either high-power (expanding their body to take up more space with arms and legs out wide) or low-power poses (bringing their limbs closer to the centre of their body). After two minutes, the high-power posers experienced a drop in cortisol, and the low-power posers experienced a rise in cortisol. So, for children high in cortisol (which happens when in a state of fight or flight), taking a powerful pose, standing with their hands on their hips, expanding their bodies, and standing strong like a Superhero could help decrease cortisol levels.

Again, remember, at times, 'flight' is a very sensible response. In certain dangerous situations, getting away from the crisis is crucial. However, in everyday life, avoidance can have a negative impact on a child's ability to live a full life.

☼ Top Tip!

For a child who tends to go into a flight response, supporting them to register safety is all important. A mantra such as 'I am safe and secure' or 'I am calm, and all is well' can help a child register safety.

Freeze is a form of numbness. It can be a child who appears startled when under pressure or a child who shuts down when anxiety hits. This child can tend to disengage or zone out of reality. As they tend to shut down when anxious, they find decision-making difficult and may daydream or disassociate from reality. Parents may say their child has their head in the clouds. Physically, the child can appear unable to move or look away from the source of the threat. They may become mute with fear. Often, in the freeze response, a child can rely on dissociation to detach themselves from the danger. They struggle to concentrate, to listen to others, or to think clearly. A child in this response will find it difficult to absorb information, for example, in the classroom.

If a child has a triggered freeze response, the key is to provide a sense of safety. Placing an object in front of the child to focus on can help, as it can allow the child to come back to the present. You can use a calm voice to reassure them you are present but allow them time to return to focus on their environment.

☝ Give it a Try!

When a child experiences the freeze response, it can help to engage their senses. The 5-4-3-2-1 Grounding Technique can be helpful. In this, you ask the child to think of:

- Five things you can see around you.
- Four things you can touch around you.
- Three things you can hear.
- Two things you can smell.
- One thing you can taste.

A quick alternative can be to give them some peppermint to taste or some lavender to smell.

Fawn is the final trauma response and is the one that people are often less familiar with. Fawn presents as people pleasing and compliance. The child has learned safety by putting the needs of others before their own. They aim always to please others, may struggle with perfectionism, and have difficulty saying no. Parents may say that their child is compliant or easily led. This is a child who appears very polite and agreeable. They do not want to offend or draw attention to themselves. This child may have difficulty saying 'no' and you may notice that they always apologise. They are often very aware of the emotions of others while neglecting their own needs. Fawning is not just being considerate or kind, it can be a response rooted in trauma.

Children who have a triggered fawn response are more likely to go under the radar. These are the children who cope with their anxiety by always trying to please others and avoid confrontation. Our role is to help them find their voice. We want to support them in having their needs heard. Modelling healthy conflict resolution and healthy boundary setting can help these children find their own voice.

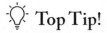 **Top Tip!**

As fawn is primarily a people-pleasing response, it can be helpful to role-play situations with your child where they would prefer to stand their ground. Say they want to become more assertive in their relationship with their best friend. You can role-play situations where they would like to get across their viewpoint so they can practise clarifying their needs.

It can be helpful to talk to your child about these responses to threats. If your child understands that there is a scientific reason behind their behaviour, it can help them better understand their responses and be kinder to themselves. Knowing that there is a reason for the physiological changes they are experiencing and knowing that there are tools they can use when these responses take over their bodies can help them feel more empowered to deal with their anxiety.

It can also help to keep an eye on possible triggers that are initiating this response in your child. If you can identify a pattern of triggers, it can help to understand the everyday stressors that have become exaggerated in your child's mind. Both physical dangers and psychological stressors can trigger the fight-flight-freeze-fawn response. Here are some common triggers that can initiate this response in children:

- Confrontation – both with other children and authority figures.
- New interactions and new activities – the demands of interactions with new people and activities they are not familiar with can be overwhelming.
- Academic expectations – for some children, the expectations of the school setting can be triggering.
- Transitions – moving from one activity to another or from one place to another can trigger change and unpredictability for children.
- Sensory overload – sensory issues can result in complete over-whelm for children sensitive to sensory stimulation (visual, auditory, touch, movement, olfactory, gustatory).
- Hunger, thirst, tiredness – all these physical needs can push a child into a stress response.

I must finish this section by acknowledging that some children have experienced serious trauma in their lives. If your child has been exposed to trauma, for example, bereavement within the family or serious illness, which you feel is the cause of their anxiety, then professional help should be sought. Some children will also face encounters in life which can be anxiety-provoking, particularly for children who have a predisposition towards anxious responses, for example, a change of school, parental separation, or friendship issues. These challenges may also provoke a period of anxiety. We often say as parents that all we want for our children is that they are happy. We cannot ever guarantee happiness for our children. Instead, we can support them to develop the skills they need to cope with life's inevitable challenges.

The Brain-Gut Link

The Central Nervous System (CNS) consists of the brain and the spinal cord. It is referred to as 'central' as it coordinates activities such as thought, movement, and emotion across the whole body. It also controls our heart rate, breathing and body temperature. The gut lining is known as the Enteric Nervous System (ENS). It comprises two thin layers of over one hundred million nerve cells lining the gastrointestinal tract. Studies show that although the brain can contribute to stomach issues (think of 'butterflies in your stomach,' having a 'gut-wrenching' experience, or 'going with your gut instinct'), irritation in the gastrointestinal system can also send signals to the CNS that impact on mood.

Scientists are increasingly noting a link between what happens in our brains and what happens in our gut. There has been a strong focus on the Vagus nerve, which emerges from the brain stem and links to all the main organs in the body. This nerve oversees several bodily functions such as mood, digestion, immune response, and reflex anxiety such as coughing and sneezing. Vagus means wanderer in Latin, which is very appropriate as this nerve is said to wander down the body carrying a range of signals from the brain to the organs.

The Vagus nerve provides a link through which the brain sends information to the gut and receives information in reverse. By sending information from the brain stem back to the body, it helps to control the heart rate, digestion, and the immune system. For this reason, it is sometimes called an 'information superhighway.' It is part of our parasympathetic nervous system and is responsible for calming our bodies. It is often referred to as the 'rest and digest' system, compared to the sympathetic nervous system, which is linked to our body's stress response. It can trigger a relaxation response in the body, slowing our heart rate and calming our nervous system down. This increases something called vagal tone, which is the activity and effectiveness of the Vagus nerve.

There is evidence from research that stimulating the Vagus nerve can support people with depression, autoimmune disorders, PTSD, and epilepsy. The largest clinical trial undertaken so far in examining the impact of Vagus nerve stimulation on patients with depression is currently underway in the United States. However, previous research investigated the impact of cold stimulation applied to participants' necks and found that it slowed down their heart rates[14]. Another study found similar results, showing drinking ice-cold water slowed participants' heart rates[15]. Advocates argue that there are many everyday ways in which we can stimulate the Vagus nerve to support overall mental wellbeing.

This area of research is relatively young in psychological terms. However, there are many ways in which we can try to improve our vagal tone at home. I should make it clear that these are not all clinically proven. Indeed, we still have a lot to learn about the brain-gut connection. However, we know that this system acts to counterbalance the fight-flight-freeze-fawn system and can trigger a relaxation response in our body, so it is worth considering in terms of how we can support our children.

We know mindfulness, slow breathing techniques, and general exercise all help improve Vagal tone. Other recommended techniques range from loud gargling with water, singing out loud, and tapping exercises where you tap on your chest or face. Cold water immersion, either face only or cold showers, is also suggested. Massaging any part of the body, but particularly the feet, is advocated by many. Finally, laughter is recommended too. We may need a little more research to confirm the effectiveness of some of the above, but they are ideas that would be easy to incorporate into our everyday lives and those of our children.

Finally, it is important to note that as much of our gut microbiome is influenced by our diet, we can also make positive changes in terms of diet, which can support positive gut health. There is a variety of foods that are recommended to support good gut health. These include yoghurt with live cultures, sauerkraut, almonds, avocados, leafy greens, and green tea. Probiotics are found in many of these foods and can also be taken as probiotic supplements to aid the development of good gut bacteria.

Conclusion

As parents, we often question ourselves as to why our children struggle with anxiety. We try to build a loving environment for our children, so we worry that we have failed them somehow if the world feels unsafe for them. However, sometimes, the fear your child is experiencing is not based on real-life threats, and there is an error of judgment involved. Some of our children overestimate the risks they face while also underestimating their ability to cope with these risks. But, once we know how to support them, we can work towards a much healthier approach to life's challenges. Talking to them about anxiety and what is happening in their brains and bodies when they feel anxious is the first step in this process.

CHAPTER 3

Types of Anxiety

There is nothing either good or bad,
but thinking makes it so.

William Shakespeare

We know many of our children will experience periods of worry or anxiety, very often caused by everyday family experiences. But, if a period of anxiety continues and impacts the child's ability to lead their everyday home, school, or social life, or if a child does not outgrow the expected worries typical of a certain period of development, then we need to look a little deeper. It can be helpful to understand the various types of anxiety our child may be experiencing.

The Diagnostic and Statistical Manual of Mental Disorders 5th Edition (DSM5) identifies a range of anxiety disorders that we might typically come across in children. These include Separation Anxiety, Selective Mutism, Social Anxiety Disorder, Specific Phobia, Panic Disorder, and Generalised Anxiety Disorder. I am also going to mention Obsessive Compulsive Disorder, School-Based Anxiety, and Anxiety About World Events, as these are three areas which are becoming increasingly common among children and teens.

Separation Anxiety

We understand that a child's primary attachment figure provides a sense of security to the young child, so it is a normal response from many children in early childhood to fear separation from their parents or caregivers. In fact, at certain stages of development, separation anxiety is to be expected. It can start at about 7-8 months old and often peak at about 12-18 months. These children can respond very vocally when their parent even tries to leave the room and may cry or cling to the parent if they fear being separated from them. This is an important developmental stage, as the child has formed a healthy attachment and shows that they don't want to be away from you. This fear usually leaves gradually during early childhood as your child becomes more secure in their understanding that you will return and all will be well in their world again.

 From the Horse's Mouth

I am always an advocate for reading to children about topics they are struggling with or challenges they are facing. My favourite three books to read to children to support their understanding of their connection to us are:

Owl Babies by Martin Waddell. An old family favourite. Sarah, Percy, and Bill wake up one night to find their mother gone from their nest. Bill is very worried, and Sarah and Percy do their best to comfort him while they wait. When she returns, she reassures them she will always come back to them.

The Invisible String by Patrice Karst. Jeremy and Liza's mum reassures them that even though she might not be with them, they are all connected by an invisible string. Even though they cannot see it with their eyes, they can feel it in their heart. Whenever they miss her, her love travels along the string, reminding them of this important connection.

The Kissing Hand by Audrey Penn. Chester Raccoon is nervous about starting school. After reassuring him about new friends and toys, his mum kisses him on his paw. She tells him to put his paw to his cheek whenever he misses her and knows her love will be with him wherever he goes.

However, some children may develop separation anxiety older than this, and for many of these children, it is precipitated by a change in routine or a transition in their lives that they find stressful. Maybe starting preschool or primary school, moving house, or even the arrival of a new sibling. As parents, it fills us with anxiety to see our children struggling in this way. When we see our children filled with fear, our instinct is to scoop them up in our arms and protect them. But this will often make our children feel they were right to be anxious about the separation. Instead, the most important thing for children at times of transition is our calm, reassuring presence. Your connection with your child is the most important support you can give. Remember, the anxiety is caused by the threat the child feels at being parted from you. So, by retaining a connection with you, the anxiety is reduced.

Transitional objects are a great way for the child to maintain that loving connection to their secure base. A transitional object is any object from home or family life that bridges the connection between the home and the environment they are transitioning to. They support the child in navigating separation from those closest to them. They range from teddies to blankies to significant objects such as special lockets or gemstones. Very often, there is a sensory aspect to the object, whether it be the softness of a cuddly toy or the soothing sensation of a round stone. The objects lessen the stress of separation while also soothing and comforting the child. They invite emotional wellbeing.

👆 Give it a Try!

Here are two ideas for using transitional objects to bridge the gap between home and preschool/school:

Matching Love Hearts:
Draw a little heart on your wrist and a matching one on theirs. If they miss you during the day or feel the need to connect with you, they put their fingers on the little heart. They will feel their pulse, like a reassuring heartbeat, when they touch their wrist. Let them know you will press your love heart if you miss them. You can also add a spray of your perfume or aftershave to their wrist as another little connection to you.

Pebble in my Pocket:
Find two similar pebbles, gemstones, or crystals. You keep one in your pocket, and the child keeps the other in their pocket. Tell them that any time they feel a little nervous or are missing you, they give their pebble a little squeeze. It is a very concrete reminder of their connection to you. Some alternatives to a pebble they might like to keep in their pocket are a little photo of mum/dad/family or a hankie with your perfume/aftershave on it.

Don't be worried about a child's reliance on a transitional object. Research tells us that they foster independence and security, help children transition to new settings, and ease anxiety in new situations.

Then, while those objects are doing their work, the second way to support a child is by building a loving connection with a new adult - another attachment that brings security to the child. Whether this is an educator at preschool, at primary school, or another trusted adult they are in the care of, the goal is to build a sense of safety with that person. Educators are very aware of the need to develop strong, loving relationships with the children in their care. In education, we often speak about professional love and how a child can only learn once they feel held in the loving presence of the educator.

I remember an Early Years Educator telling me once that if mums are upset as their children struggle with separation, she always reminds them that this means they are a great mum. Their child loves them and their home so much that they don't want to be parted from them. I thought it was such an empathetic way to support a parent dealing with a very challenging situation.

Give it a Try!

Supporting our children with separation anxiety involves not only considering the context they are moving into but, often, more importantly, their struggle with separation from us. Building a bridge between the home and educational context can help. Here are a few steps you can take to smooth this transition.

- Start by focusing on your connection with your child. This can help you lead them towards the transition. Use playfulness to engage with them, for example, using the same little play rituals or routines every day leading up to the transition.
- Validate their emotions by acknowledging any big emotions without judgement or expectation about what they 'should' be feeling. Just listening to their feelings helps, as the fear of separation that they feel is very real to them.
- At the point of separation, make clear your connection to their 'caretaker'. Seeing a strong connection between you and that trusted adult is important in terms of security for the child.

- Use transitional objects, as described above, to support them during separation. These provide a very concrete reminder of your love.
- Remind them of their return to you. This could be a reminder of when you will collect them or what you will do together on collection.

Remember, the most important thing for children at times of transition is having 'one good adult' in their lives. Someone they can rely on to be a calm, reassuring presence. This is a very strong protective factor for our children's wellbeing.

Selective Mutism

Selective Mutism (SM) is an anxiety disorder where a child cannot talk in certain contexts, usually in school or maybe with extended family members. However, they can speak to those closest to them, family and close friends, sometimes children rather than adults. These children speak fluently in some situations but remain silent in others. The condition is known to begin early in life and can be temporary, such as during a hospital stay, but in most cases, it may persist and last right through a child's school life. Although the term 'selective' might suggest that the child 'selects' not to speak, this is not the case. These children are not choosing silence. Their anxiety is heightened, and they just cannot talk. It is a bit like stage fright. They are physically frozen.

Starting preschool or school can be a trigger for many children. Sometimes teachers think the child is just shy, or they think the child has great self-control that they can manage to stop themselves talking all day long. But this is not about self-control. Children with SM desperately want to speak and join in with others but find themselves physically unable to do so due to their anxiety.

It is important to try not to label the child as 'non-speaking' in front of other people or punish them in any way for remaining silent, as this will only increase anxiety. Instead, parents can encourage the child to take baby steps out of their comfort zone, such as whispering a few words to extended family. Imaginative play and puppet play can help as some children may speak when 'in role.'

Treatment for SM focuses on lowering the anxiety that the child has for speaking in a particular setting. This can involve play therapy, which allows children to express their experiences and feelings. The *Sliding in Technique* is also known to be helpful in the classroom. This is where one person gains the trust of the child. Once the child is at ease and can communicate with that person, another person, often another child, is gradually introduced into the situation. Shaping can also be helpful, where the child is encouraged to interact nonverbally before being slowly coaxed into trying sounds, then whispering, and gradually trying a word or two.

⚙ Ask The Expert

I asked Lucy Nathanson, Child Therapist, founder of Confidentchildren.co.uk and expert in Selective Mutism[16], what advice she has for parents of children with SM:

'As a specialist in Selective Mutism, I regularly get asked, 'Will my child grow out of Selective Mutism? Should I give them time?' It is typical for children to need some time to settle into school. However, if a child is not talking to adults or peers after the first month of school, then they need support with this. Contrary to common belief, it is not that children will start talking by themselves if they are given time; children do not usually grow out of Selective Mutism. Imagine a child who hasn't spoken at school for a few days versus a child who hasn't spoken for a few months or years. The longer they haven't spoken, the more entrenched the Selective Mutism becomes. It becomes part of their identity. Others begin to label them as 'the person who doesn't talk,' and they begin to self-identify in this way.

In the case of Selective Mutism, early intervention is key. Children can absolutely overcome Selective Mutism. We see it happen all the time. But we shouldn't wait to see if they grow out of it. A person can be supported in overcoming Selective Mutism at any age. However, it is ideal if they can get support when they are young. Supporting a child in overcoming Selective Mutism can take time and patience, but there are proven strategies and techniques that can be implemented to help. Learn about Selective Mutism, arrange a meeting to include the parent and the school to put a plan in place to help the child as soon as possible, and enlist the support of a therapist trained in Selective Mutism if you can. It can feel like a long road, but every little step your child takes is a huge leap, and one day you'll look back and see how far they've come.'

Social Anxiety

Social anxiety is an intense fear of social situations, usually including a fear of personal humiliation and judgement. Social anxiety makes it more difficult to engage in social situations, whether going to family events or situations like reading out loud in class. Although children with social anxiety appear to be comfortable in situations with friends or family, issues arise in situations with less familiar people or situations where they feel they might be 'on show'. Before engaging in social situations that they find difficult, they will often experience high levels of anxiety. They will often try to avoid any situations where they feel they might be judged about themselves or their performance.

From the Horse's Mouth

I remember my daughter's sports day in her first year of school. She didn't want to take part in the running race. I couldn't understand why because she was a great little runner. But I could see that she was uncomfortable. After the race, I asked her why she didn't want to run. Parents were standing on the sides of the running track, and she felt that they were all watching her. I tried to explain that they were watching their own children and that they honestly weren't bothered about anyone but their own child. But she felt they were all looking at her. It was only later, as she became more anxious about other situations, I looked back at this and realised it was the beginning of her fearful thoughts.

Social anxiety is more prominent as adolescence starts, meaning anytime from approximately ten years onwards. This is usually when we become aware of it as parents. In fact, experiencing social anxieties is a typical part of adolescent development. During those years, it is normal for our children to become more concerned with judgement from others, particularly their peers. One of the roles of the adolescent period is to figure out your own identity, so our young teens will often become preoccupied with considering their role in life. This is to be expected. But it is also a time when social pressures are very high, and peer groups may be less understanding than they were in younger years. The transition to secondary school can also be a trigger for social anxiety as the teen moves from the primary school setting, which places less demand on them, to the more socially and emotionally demanding secondary school environment.

☝ Give it a Try!

If you are worried that your child may be struggling with social anxiety, these questions may help you to consider this further:

- Do they tend to try to blend into the background in social situations?
- Do they try to avoid group activities?
- Do they worry about being judged by their peers?
- Do they blush or become awkward in new situations?
- Do they avoid expressing their own opinion in public?
- Do they struggle to make their own needs known to strangers?
- Do they worry about someone making fun of them?
- Do they worry excessively about what others think of them?
- Do they become embarrassed speaking in public?
- Do they tend to miss out on social events due to nervousness?

Most children and teens can feel socially anxious every now and then. But social anxiety disorder is not something that a child feels occasionally. These emotions occur daily. The child may spend every day in school caught in a cycle of anxiety, worrying about the judgement of their peers, then come home every day exhausted by the demands of 'keeping up appearances' in the school setting.

A common fear for children or teens with social anxiety is that others will know how uncomfortable they feel. The child will try to hide their feelings, but if they think others know they are anxious, they may blush. Blushing is a physiological response to a stressful or embarrassing situation. Many children with social anxiety will blush, particularly if they are put on the spot, they feel that people are looking at them, or they are the centre of attention. The process of blushing is automatic, so it is almost impossible to stop once it has begun. The child is then usually embarrassed by the blush, and the more embarrassed they are, the redder they typically get.

Many children with social anxiety will try to avoid situations that are socially demanding. They are worried that if they speak up in class, they will make a fool of themselves. They are worried that if they arrive late to a party, everyone will turn around and look at them as they enter the room. They are worried that if they take part in a sporting event, they will fall and embarrass themselves. They are worried that if they talk to a girl they like, she will laugh at them. The problem is that if they avoid doing any of these things, they will never challenge those flawed beliefs and prove them wrong. By not trying out these situations, they never learn that they can cope with minor embarrassment. This can result in losing all confidence in taking social risks and instead choosing to avoid them. But, with avoidance comes restriction. If we avoid everything in society that makes us anxious, we can end up retreating from society, and we do not want that for our children and teens.

A diagnosis of Agoraphobia is given when Social Phobia becomes so embedded that it results in the individual refusing to engage in any social situations, often becoming housebound. This diagnosis is not very common in young children but is more commonly seen in older teens or young adults. The teen will often withdraw to a setting where they feel safest, usually their home or their room. These children will usually need professional support to help them overcome this issue.

Reassuring your child that there is no danger in social situations often achieves nothing. Instead, you want to try to do something which can make them question if their fears are grounded. We want to encourage them to both notice and challenge these negative thoughts.

Normalising mistakes and imperfections can be helpful in changing the core beliefs of an anxious child. Those who struggle with social anxiety often see themselves as being in the spotlight. They feel that everyone is aware of their behaviour and judges them against an impossible standard. If we can normalise imperfection, it can help our children see that most people are fearful of certain situations. Many other children will feel anxious before reading in class, making eye contact with the school principal, or, if they are older, giving a class presentation or taking part in a school play. Their anxiety may be heightened, but others have the same challenges. Often, their classmates are so engrossed in their own lives that they don't notice the mistakes of others. If they do, they move on very quickly, and your child's 'mistake' is soon forgotten.

Specific Phobia

Phobias are intense fears of situations or objects others consider unharmful, such as small spiders. Many young children have mild fears about triggers such as travelling in a lift, injections, and particular animals. But as they get older, if the fear intensifies to the extent that it is interfering with their day-to-day life, it is considered a phobia.

There are generally five categories of specific phobias:

- Animals (spiders, snakes, dogs)
- Natural Environment (heights, water, fire)
- Blood and Injections (needles, medical or dental procedures)
- Situational (flying, enclosed spaces, lifts)
- Other (phobias that don't fit into the previous categories)

Although many children would have some fears that fall within the above categories, when these become a phobia, they can be debilitating. Often, the child will go out of their way to avoid what makes them anxious. Supporting a child who has a phobia usually involves taking baby steps towards coping with what they are avoiding. This cannot be done without some degree of discomfort. But the benefits of tackling the phobia can be life-changing for the child.

If we notice a child beginning to express nerves about a particular situation, it can help to try to acclimatise them to the situation early before minor worries develop into stronger fears. We can see this in the example below.

⚙ Ask the Expert

One fear that quite a few children experience is of the dentist. I asked Dr Niall Neeson (also known as The Calming Dentist[17]), who runs the Dental Fear Solutions programme at the award-winning Boyne Dental Clinic, about how we can support these children. He advises: 'There are lots of things we can do as parents to help our kids develop a positive relationship with dentistry. Although dentistry has progressed a lot over the years, remember that at the beginning, it's still a highly unusual environment and situation for your child. Think about the clinical appearance of the room, the bright lights, and a stranger wanting to poke around your mouth. Paying attention to preparing your child for their visit goes a long way. In a relaxed, matter-of-fact way, we can explain what will happen. Something like, 'We're going to see Niall the dentist today. He's going to count your teeth and help teach us how to keep them strong and healthy.' Get them interested by asking, 'How many teeth do you think you have?' Reading books to your child about going to the dentist can be a wonderful way of learning what to expect and allowing them to prepare a positive image in their imagination. Try 'We're going to the dentist' from the 'Big Steps' series.

Modelling can work well. If you are comfortable visiting the dentist or hygienist, then bring them along. They could observe you or their siblings from the corner of the room. When they see their family doing it, they'll probably want to have a go on the chair, too. Nothing beats getting into a routine and habit of attending from a young age. Would you believe the official advice is to attend the dentist before the age of one? That visit could simply be sitting on your knee, but getting in early will help normalise it. Building confidence can really pay off in helping to keep their dental journey smooth moving forward.'

Panic Disorder

Panic disorder is probably one of the most severe forms of anxiety. A child who develops a panic disorder will experience panic attacks involving feelings of terror, with physical symptoms such as heart palpitations, dizziness, nausea, and the feeling that they might die. Essentially, the threat response kicks in for no reason, stimulating fear, which is particularly frightening for children as it comes out of the blue.

Panic attacks are more common than most of us realise, with approximately 30% of adults experiencing a panic attack at some point in their lives. For many adults, they usually occur at periods of great stress. When they happen, they are extremely distressing. They involve an abrupt onset of panic that reaches a peak within a few minutes and includes at least four of the following symptoms:

- Fear of dying
- Pounding heart
- Trembling or shaking
- Shortness of breath
- Chest pain or discomfort
- Nausea
- Light-headedness
- Chills or shivers
- Fear of losing control
- Paraesthesia (numbness or tingling sensations)
- Derealisation (feelings of unreality) or depersonalisation (detachment)

Many people report that a panic attack feels like what they imagine a heart attack to feel like. They feel as if their chest is going to explode. They struggle to breathe properly and are sure they are going to die. Even taking small breaths can be a struggle, and the person will often start hyperventilating.

During a panic attack, your body is being fuelled by adrenaline. As it rushes through your bloodstream, you are left feeling frozen in a state of negative anticipation. Small amounts of adrenaline can be positive, contributing to feelings of excitement and exhilaration. However, when it becomes excessive, it fuels anxiety, leading to racing thoughts, feelings of dread, and catastrophic thinking.

It is extremely distressing to see a child have a panic attack, but it is very important to stay calm. Use a gentle, soothing voice to encourage them to take deep breaths and reassure them that the panic will be over soon. Taking deep breaths along with them while encouraging them to do the same can help. For some children, a comfort object, maybe a cuddly toy or a family pet, can help them to shift their focus from the panic. For others, visualising their 'happy place,' somewhere they feel safe, can help.

Once the panic subsides, your child will need plenty of time to calm down. Again, your soothing presence will help during this time. Afterwards, speaking to them about panic attacks and the science behind anxiety can help allay some of their fears. Knowing the facts behind these attacks, that they are common, are not actually dangerous, and that they will subside, can help. But, if your child is experiencing persistent panic attacks, it is recommended that you seek professional support.

Give it a Try!

If your child is in a state of panic, a small step can help bring them out of that fight or flight state. Chartered Psychologist

Dr Julie Smith recommends taking two ice cubes and getting the child to clench them in the palm of their hands. The act of holding the cold ice is like a jolt to the system. It brings the child back to being present in their body while also lowering body temperature and heart rate. Your child's body and brain are moved from focusing on the panic to concentrating instead on the sensation of coldness. You can also take ice cubes and run them along the inside of your child's arm, or, for an older child or teen, you can get them to hold a cube of ice in their mouth, telling them to try to hold it against the roof of their mouth. An ice cube is not a permanent solution to anxiety, but it can be helpful for short-term relief in acute situations.

Generalised Anxiety Disorder

Generalised Anxiety Disorder (GAD) involves excessive worry that occurs most days about several different issues (for example, school performance, health issues, car accidents) that the child struggles to control. It is not that they worry about different things to other children. The issue is that they worry much more. They are also more likely to worry about remote events that may never happen compared to real problems they face. The child may appear to have an intolerance of uncertainty. They can also experience tiredness, irritability, poor concentration, difficulties with memory, and sleep difficulties linked to their anxiety. As compared to a brief period of worry, GAD usually involves excessive anxiety that the child finds difficult to control, occurring for more than six months. It causes them real distress and impairs their ability to function normally.

A crucial point to remember about GAD is that most children have periods of anxiety. However, if your child's worry is becoming excessive, intense worrying thoughts happen every day, or they find it difficult to control these thoughts that have been taking place over a prolonged period, then they may be struggling with GAD. In this case, you might want to speak to your GP for further clarification.

So many parents I have spoken to who would consider their child to have GAD have said to me that from an early age, they would have considered their child to be 'a worrier'. Their child has been unable to tell them what they are worried about, or they have a wide range of issues they tend to worry about. These children seem to be caught in a cycle of anxiety, which they struggle to break free from. The causes of the anxiety might not seem logical to us as parents. But just because anxiety is not logical does not make it any less real. It might not make sense to us, but that does not mean it is not a valid worry to the child.

☀ Top Tip!

Children struggling with anxiety will often take on worries that do not belong to them. Talking about what is worrying them and who each worry belongs to can help remove some weight from their shoulders. So, the worry that Mum or Dad might get sick is something we can offer to take responsibility for to help lighten their load.

GAD is usually not too difficult to spot in children, as their anxiousness can become all-consuming. These children seem to worry endlessly, and anxiety seems to dominate their lives. One of the biggest challenges for parents is that they often cannot understand how the anxiety started or what is going on with their child.

Worrying creates a false sense of control, a belief that the mere fact of worrying prepares us to cope with a problem effectively. Dr Robert Leahy, author of *The Worry Cure*[18], argues that many of us worry as we believe this will prevent something bad from happening. However, in researching anxiety in adults, he found that 85% of things that the participants in his study worried about never happened. Of the remaining 15% that did happen, almost 80% of people said that, in hindsight, they had coped better than they had expected, reminding us that, as humans, we are more resilient than we imagine. He suggests keeping a worry log, recording all your day-to-day worries, then recording afterwards if these things actually occurred, as a reminder that most of what we worry and stress about is pointless.

Obsessive Compulsive Disorder (OCD)

It is common for children to engage in small routines and rituals, which can often help them in terms of a sense of security. However, if these rituals become more than a comforting routine, and instead, the child feels that if they do not complete the ritual, something bad will happen, then we must investigate them further. OCD involves two aspects: obsessions (unwanted thoughts that cause distress – often about a bad thing happening) and compulsions (behaviours that are meant to reduce the distress – they are intended to stop the bad thing happening).

In everyday life, we often refer to being 'obsessed' with something to indicate something we really like. However, in psychological terms, an obsession is something that causes distress. When we speak about OCD, these are persistent unwanted thoughts, images, or urges that cause distress to the child experiencing them. They are usually frightening or upsetting and cause great anxiety to the child. Common obsessions include:

- *Fear of Contamination*: a fear of being contaminated by someone or something. This can include worries about germs and dirt.
- *Fear of Harm*: a fear that either the child or their loved ones will come to harm. Often, this can involve a sense of guilt for even thinking that something bad could happen to a loved one.

- *Fear of Causing Harm or Violence*: this involves thoughts that the child themselves could harm someone else or that they are a danger to others (but does not mean that they would, in fact, hurt others).
- *Fearful Taboo Thoughts:* these are unwanted thoughts involving sex, religion, or harm.

Compulsions are the repeated behaviours a child engages in when they feel the distress of obsessions. Here are some compulsions that are quite common for children with OCD:

- *Compulsive Counting*: this involves completing a task a specific number of times, often counting numbers in their head without others noticing, for example, having to flick a light switch three times.
- *Compulsive Checking*: a child might need to keep checking that you locked the door when you left the house or that they turned their bedroom light off.
- *Compulsive Ordering*: this could be seen in a child who needs to have items in their bedroom in specific places and is upset if friends or family move items from their designated place.
- *Compulsive Repeating*: your child might have to repeat certain words or behaviours to themselves in a set sequence. Any disruption to the sequence can cause distress.
- *Compulsive Cleaning*: this might involve continued washing of hands, needing to disinfect after touching public surfaces, or removing their 'dirty' school uniform as soon as they arrive home.

These compulsions are often time-consuming and are a direct response aimed at alleviating the distress caused by the obsession. The more a child engages in compulsive behaviour, the more embedded the obsession becomes.

OCD is usually characterised by irrational beliefs. For example, the belief that touching a door handle will cause the child to get sick and die. However, sometimes, it is characterised by distorted beliefs. For example, touching a door handle is 'gross' and 'disgusting', so the child will avoid doing this at all costs. Irrational beliefs can be easier to treat than distorted beliefs. A therapist can disprove that touching a door handle will cause you to get sick and die. It is harder to challenge a distorted belief, as they are an extreme interpretation of a belief that seems acceptable. Trying to persuade the child that touching the door handle is not gross can be difficult, as there is some limited basis for the child to argue that their belief has some logical foundation. The child will often not see any compelling reason to challenge their beliefs or behaviour.

When coping with OCD, often, a child will use safety behaviours. These short-term relief strategies come into play when the child feels highly anxious - for example, using a tissue to avoid touching a door handle, wearing gloves to avoid contact with germs, or sitting in the back row of the classroom. They may also use avoidant behaviours to avoid situations that cause anxiety, such as avoiding shaking hands with anyone, refusing to use public bathrooms, or refusing to eat in public spaces.

Cognitive Behavioural Therapy is recognised as the gold standard treatment for OCD and would usually include exposure response therapy. This therapy can cause discomfort to the child and involves a degree of motivation for treatment. It involves engaging in a series of tasks whereby the child slowly confronts their anxiety by exposing the child to their obsessions and supporting them to learn not to engage in their compulsions. The belief is that by not doing what the OCD is telling the child to do, they learn to tolerate manageable levels of discomfort. Over time, the child regains a sense of empowerment over the OCD compulsions.

 From the Horse's Mouth

Talking to your child about OCD and explaining it to them at their developmental level can help. Here are some books I have found to be helpful for children and teens about OCD:

- If you have a younger child (approx. 5-13 years) who you feel is struggling with OCD-like tendencies, I recommend a book called 'What to Do When Your Brain Gets Stuck: A Kids Guide to Overcoming OCD' by Dawn Huebner.
- Again, for the younger age group, a good choice is 'Up and Down the Worry Hill: A Children's Book about Obsessive Compulsive Disorder and Its Treatment' by Dr Aureen Pinto Wagner.
- For children approximately 6-12 years, 'The OCD Workbook for Kids: Skills to Help Manage Obsessive Thoughts and Compulsive Behaviours, An Instant Help Book for Parents and Kids' by Anthony Puliafico is an evidence-based workbook that can help.
- For older children, 'Free From OCD: A Workbook for Teens with Obsessive Compulsive Disorder' by Timothy Sisemore outlines forty cognitive behavioural exercises to help with OCD.

School-Based Anxiety

For many children, school is where they cheerfully engage in learning opportunities and make new friends. Others may not necessarily enjoy all their time at school, but they continue to learn and grow. However, for some, anxiety about attending school is increasingly becoming an issue. This anxiety is experienced in different ways by different children. Some experience mild anxiety, which they deal with in the morning while facing the prospect of school. However, at the other end of the scale, this is a much more stressful experience, and school has become traumatic for these children.

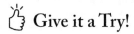 Give it a Try!

For children with *mild* school anxiety, this activity can not only help you to gain an understanding of the specific worries that a child may have about going to school but can also help them to 'park' some of those worries with you for the day, allowing them space to breathe in the school environment.

Worries in My Pocket:
Talk to your child about any concerns they have about school. Write the worries down on pieces of paper. Then you put the pieces of paper in your pocket. Tell your child you will carry their worries for the day while they are in school, so they don't have to carry them alone.

When your child comes home from school, you can take out the worries and talk through them. Often, some of those worries will never happen during the day, which can give your child some perspective.

In the school context, there are various ways anxiety can present. Anxiety in the classroom can present as a child who struggles with attendance, is unlikely to ask for support, may not wish to speak or read in class, and may struggle to take in information. Some children listen to every word from the teacher, anxiously working on what they have been instructed to do, trying to achieve perfection. This is the child who will keep erasing their work, worried it is never good enough. Or you can have a child who is not hearing a word the teacher says. Instead, they might be thinking about an experience in the playground earlier at break time, worried that their friend was playing with someone else, and asking themselves a million questions about what it could mean. We call this *ruminating* when our children tend to go over and over past or future events, imagining what bad things might occur. This is often linked to *catastrophising*, a tendency to interpret events negatively without any real evidence to support that interpretation. These two can often go hand in hand. A child will go over events repeatedly, anticipating all the possible negative developments which may occur, each time coming up with a worse conclusion.

Children with school anxiety may also present with constant physical complaints, stomach aches, headaches, and tiredness. Often, they have attendance issues.

As parents, it is important to remember that the demands of school are many, and outside of their home, school is where children spend most of their time. The expectations are not only academic, but there are numerous social and emotional demands on the child, from peer relationships, teacher relationships, organisational skills, juggling various demands, being put on display in the classroom, and conforming to the unwritten rules of the school. There are also the demands of the playground, where they mix with large groups of children and cope with complex social expectations. It is no wonder that this context can be challenging for so many children, particularly those who already have a disposition to anxious thoughts. Children must exert a huge effort to sit still, pay attention, follow directions, and engage with the teacher in a meaningful way. They are also doing all this without their *one good adult,* the parents or carers who are their safe space, the ones they depend on.

The first thing a parent needs to try to uncover is the issues specifically impacting their child. Speaking to them in simple terms can help to get an understanding of their anxious expectations.

☝ Give it a Try!

If your child cannot explain what it is about school that is making them feel anxious, it can help to ask them what they would change about school if they had a magic wand.

If they had a magic wand...

- Would they have a new teacher?
- Would they move seats in the classroom?
- Would they change the bathrooms?
- Would they have less homework?
- Would they change anything about friendships?

Giving them the opportunity to tell you what they would change is a great starting point for conversations about what is making them unhappy. This can help you uncover the issues causing them most stress in the school situation.

I mentioned above that school anxiety can be quite severe in some children. This more formal form of school anxiety is often referred to as school refusal. This is another term I take issue with as it suggests that the child refuses to go to school. Instead, the issue with school anxiety is that the child cannot face the school environment for distinct reasons. Perhaps they had a difficult experience in the past, or the child is struggling with a learning difficulty, and the challenges and expectations of the classroom are difficult to cope with. For so many of these children, the reason is anxiety-based. They may feel anxious about separation from their primary carer, anxious about the academic expectations placed on them, or anxious about fitting in.

Learning From Psychology

Maslow's Hierarchy of Needs is a psychological model that helps us to understand what children need most and which needs come first. It is often presented as a pyramid, with our most basic **physiological needs** at the bottom. These basic needs include food, water, and warmth. Rising to the next level is our need for **safety**. Above safety comes **love and belonging**, followed by **self-esteem**, and finally, at the top of the pyramid is **self-actualisation**. An important thing to note as the tiers progress upwards is that each tier is dependent on the needs of the lower tier being met first. Clearly, the model is a simplification of the complexity of modern life, and there is some overlap between levels. However, it reminds us that before a child can feel safe, their physiological need for food and rest comes first. Once they feel safe, they can connect with others and have their relationship needs met. Once they experience love and connection, they can fully experience good self-esteem. At the top of the pyramid, self-actualisation is the ability to reach your full potential. Maslow's Hierarchy of Needs makes clear that children can only succeed at school when their physical needs are met and when they feel safe, secure, respected, and valued in that setting. Maslow reminds us that for a child to feel part of a school community, they need to have supportive and trusting relationships within that setting.

For some children, school anxiety is not as visible within the school context but instead when they come home. These children spend their time working hard to meet the expectations and challenges of the classroom while holding in their true emotions. When they come home to you – their safe space – all their feelings are released. They might be angry, tearful, or seem disrespectful. But remember, they are physically and emotionally exhausted. We call it *After School Restraint Collapse*.

Imagine you have a can of lemonade in your hand, and you shake, shake, and shake it again. What happens when you open it? The lemonade will explode out of the can because of the pressure it has been under. Think of this when you imagine your child sitting in school all day, keeping down their emotions, holding in their anxiety, and suppressing their own needs as they conform to the role of the school child. Then, they come home to you, their safe space, and what happens? All those unmet needs release and explode out when they come in the door to you, just like the can of lemonade.

What can we do to help? First, try food, water, and rest. Also, validate their emotions. You can do this by saying something as simple as, 'It sounds like you have had a rough day today.' Give them some quiet time, and then find a ritual to decompress. It could be listening to music or watching a favourite TV show. For some children, being active is better, and riding a bike or jumping on the trampoline would suit them. They have been juggling so many expectations that time with you in their safe space will help them cope with their overwhelm and breathe again.

☀ Top Tip!

Here are two tips that can support children with *After School Restraint Collapse*:

First, try to ensure mornings before school are a positive experience. If they feel really connected to you in the morning, they are building up the emotional fuel they need to get them through the day.

The second tip is to send them to school with little love notes in their pencil case or lunch box to remind them of their connection to you during the day. A photo of you together can be equally effective. They can look at it during the day for a little 'top up' of emotional fuel.

For older children, the transition to secondary school is a time when school anxiety is very much amplified. There are so many reasons for this. The challenges of secondary school are more complex than in primary school. There are added demands such as dealing with larger numbers of students, managing a wider range of subjects, moving between different classrooms in a wider environment, and the expectation that they will juggle more homework with different submission dates.

This brings me to a final word about school anxiety: to ensure that we, as parents, put our children's wellbeing above academic achievement. As the school report cards are being prepared at the end of every school year, we can fall back into the habit of pressuring our children. It is wonderful if a child achieves great academic grades, but let's remind ourselves that our children are so much more than numbers on a page. Let's remind ourselves that our children's future happiness, success, and mental health depend on so much more than academics. Let's remind ourselves that our children are enough just as they are. These grades do not reflect their kindness, empathy, or the values they carry in their heart. Let's put away the report cards, remind ourselves what is truly important, and help them reach their full potential.

Anxiety About World Events

Naturally, news reports tend to focus on the negative things that are happening around the world. These events are newsworthy because they are unusual. We hear about world conflict, violent crimes, environmental disasters, and human catastrophes. When faced with these challenging situations that they hear about in the news, remind children that it is called *News* because it is rare. These events are reported on television and radio because they don't happen very often. The world is a wonderful place, and so many good things happen every day, but these small things are more commonplace and are not reported in the News.

In the past, we could easily turn off the TV and remove ourselves from world events. However, in our modern world, with our reliance on digital devices, it can feel as if we are surrounded by all the negativity happening across the world. For our children, particularly as they head towards their teenage years, constant access to upsetting world events can come at a cost. This reminds us of the importance of limiting our (and our children's) consumption of news items. You don't need to be inundated to be informed. Limiting family exposure to this material and countering it with more positive experiences could have a positive impact on anxiety about world events.

American television host Ted Rogers, best known for the preschool television series *Mister Rogers' Neighbourhood*, always advised that if children see news reports of difficult situations, they should be encouraged to look for helpers. For example, the doctors and nurses, the firefighters, and the everyday people who do generous and thoughtful acts as they go out of their way to help others. In every difficult situation, remind them of the helpers. Most people are good.

One form of anxiety about world events that is gaining traction is eco-anxiety. This anxiety is based on the fear of the impact of climate change on the world around us. The feeling for our children is that they cannot do anything to reverse climate change, which is a real issue. They can sometimes feel that those in power will not act on climate change and that they themselves are powerless to act. This lack of control then results in anxiety.

Speaking at the World Economic Forum in Davos in 2019, climate activist Gretta Thunberg argued that the climate crisis is the most complex challenge that humankind has ever faced. She argued that we must create transformational actions to safeguard future generations' living conditions. She told attendees, '*I don't want you to be hopeful. I want you to panic. I want you to feel the fear I feel every day. And then I want you to act. I want you to act as you would in a crisis. I want you to act as if our house is on fire. Because it is.*' Many of our children and teens would support Thunberg's call that we should panic and act as if the house is on fire.

We know that children are among those most impacted by stress about climate change. After all, it is their futures that are at stake. Promoting a connectedness to nature can help in dealing with this anxiety. We don't want our children to become so paralysed by fear about their future that they feel disempowered. Instead, we want to encourage them to care enough to take control and make small individual changes that, if enough people make them, can help reverse climate change.

A survey by the Woodland Trust in the UK in 2023 asked teens and young adults about their concerns about the future[19]. They found that one in three reported they were scared, sad, or pessimistic about climate change. However, 86% said that they felt being in nature had a positive impact on their mental health. They recommend Ecotherapy, which involves doing activities outside in nature, getting away from technology and going into a relaxing outdoor space, as a useful antidote to eco-anxiety.

☸ Ask the Expert

I asked Alex Koster, Ecotherapist, Mindfulness teacher and Nature Educator[20], for advice on supporting children and teens struggling with eco-anxiety. She advises, 'For children, one of the biggest challenges in relation to eco emotions is bridging the gap between being exposed to the magnitude of global, often abstract events and the decline of immediate immersion in their natural environment. From a developmental point of view, young children can't put world events into perspective, and they can become overwhelmed very quickly. It's hardly possible for us grown-ups to fathom all the challenges we are facing.

I am a big believer in the power of small, of local, of immediacy. Things must be tangible for children to understand. They should see first-hand how everything affects each other both positively and negatively. Nature is not optional for children. It's only here they encounter all four non-negotiable sources for their development: freedom, immediacy, resistance, and relatedness/connection. A good approach to support children with eco-anxiety is bringing them from global (in their heads) to their local natural environment. These are some tips on how to do this:

- Consciously reduce exposure to fear-inducing media coverage.
- Recognise our children's worries and take them seriously.
- Give them opportunities for multi-sensory immersion in nature.
- Involve them in actions where they can see that every small effort makes a difference, such as reducing plastic or saving energy.
- Show them examples of positive and hopeful projects.
- Support children in their creativity to come up with their own ideas.
- Integrate a regular gratitude and joy practice, bringing awareness to all the good things in our lives.
- Finally, one of the most important ways in which we can support children with eco-anxiety is by being a good role model and showing that we ourselves are proactive.'

Conclusion

There are many types of anxiety, and a child who is struggling may well experience more than one of the above to some extent. An understanding of different types of anxiety can be useful in terms of helping us to understand what our child is experiencing.

Indeed, a diagnosis or attaching a 'label' to the symptoms a child is experiencing can be helpful for some children in considering how best to support them. It can also be useful in terms of accessing support for our child. But remember, if you do get a diagnosis for your child, they are not defined by that label. It is just one aspect of who they are. They are much more than any label, as it does not reflect their various strengths and talents. Nor does it reflect their future happiness, success, and mental health.

CHAPTER 4

Breathing Deep and Finding Calm

'It's okay to be scared sometimes.' said Bear.
'Just remember, every step you take
without knowing where you're going
also means that you're brave. So very brave.'

Tara Shannon[21]

Our main goal in supporting our children who struggle with anxiety is to encourage them to find the inner bravery we know they have inside them. To encourage them to go out into the world and face their fears. But before we can do that, we need to equip them with tools they can use to self-regulate and find calm during those anxious moments. Providing simple interventions such as controlled breathing exercises can shape the emotional wellbeing of our children, helping them deal with their anxiety. They need these tools to support them as they start to see the benefits of moving beyond their comfort zones. So, let's look at how we can help them to find calm.

Finding Calm

Many of the techniques we will cover to support our children to cope in the face of anxiety relate to the *Autonomic Nervous System* in our brain. This network of nerves regulates unconscious body processes, such as our heartbeat, blood flow, breathing, and digestion. It has two branches: the *Sympathetic Nervous System* and the *Parasympathetic Nervous System*. We know that the Sympathetic system is responsible for triggering the fight or flight response. When it becomes over-stimulated, it releases disproportionate amounts of adrenaline. The Parasympathetic system helps to maintain normal bodily functions. It slows the heart rate, decreases blood pressure, and restores calm. So, the Sympathetic system mobilises the body for action, while the Parasympathetic system acts more slowly to dampen responses.

When facing a threat, the Sympathetic takes over, but once the danger has passed, we rely on the Parasympathetic system to help us return to our resting state. The Parasympathetic Nervous System is activated in many ways. We can support our children to activate this system through relaxation, mindfulness, and creating nurturing habits.

The Magic of Mindfulness

In the simplest terms, mindfulness is stopping to pay attention to what is happening in the present moment. It means being intentionally more aware of the present, even if that means simply focusing on your breath going in and out. Practicing mindfulness helps children to pause and notice their thoughts and feelings as they come and go.

When our children and teens focus on being more mindful in their lives, it can help reduce stress and increase positivity. Research has shown that being mindful helps our children stay calm under stress and is connected to emotional regulation. It also helps with cognitive development, with studies finding links to improved attention span, concentration, and focus. Mindfulness also often involves an attitude of kindness to yourself and others. Indeed, some studies report that children who engage in mindfulness are more likely to show compassion to others, help someone in need, and have better self-compassion.

Learning from Psychology

Modern brain imaging techniques are giving us a better insight into how mindfulness practise can change how different regions of the brain communicate with each other. Research from the University of Pittsburgh[22] explored the impact of mindfulness on neural pathways in the brain and found that after a course of mindfulness practice, the amygdala appeared to shrink. As it shrank, the grey matter in the pre-frontal cortex became thicker, showing increased activity in this area of higher-level thinking. Importantly, the research also found that connectivity between the amygdala and the rest of the brain decreased, while activity in the areas associated with higher-level thinking became stronger.

The more you practice being mindful, the better you get at it. And the best way to teach mindfulness to our children is to undertake it with them. We know that our children learn more from watching us than from someone simply telling them something. Mirror neurons are a relatively new phenomenon in psychology, first observed in the brains of macaque monkeys in the 1990s and more recently identified in the brains of humans. Researchers suggest that they are activated both when we perform an action ourselves and when we watch the action performed by someone else. They claim that these neurons help us to process the actions of others and learn from them. So, when our children watch us engage in a task, areas of the brain are stimulated as though the task is being performed by the child themselves. Although research into these neurons is ongoing, they seem to play an important role in how children learn to interact in a very complex social world. Reminding us that the more we model the actions we want them to develop, the easier it is for them to take them on board.

We know that our children benefit from routines and rituals. Particularly when the world feels unsafe, the predictability of routines helps a child to register safety. Try to set aside time every day to practise mindfulness together so that you are modelling how to incorporate it into their daily lives.

It can also be important to follow your child's lead. If they cannot connect with a particular practice, move on. This can be particularly important with teens, who will respond better to mindfulness if they have control over what techniques they will engage with. Studies have shown that mindfulness is not effective if it is 'forced' on a teenager. Instead, we must work to think outside the box and try different techniques to find ones that the individual child connects with and is happy to engage with. Look at the ideas below and see which are best suited to your child. However, I would encourage every parent reading this to start with *Controlled Breathing* and work with your child to develop this skill before anything else.

Controlled Breathing

The *90-Second Rule* is a term coined by Dr Jill Bolte Taylor in her book *My Stroke of Insight*[23] to explain the lifespan of negative emotions. She advises that when we react to something in our environment, this sets off a 90 second chemical process within our body during which we cannot control these reactions. Following this 90-second period, these chemicals (adrenaline and cortisol) are flushed out of our bodies. She argues that after that time, the remaining emotional and ongoing physiological response is down to our reactions to the situation. In essence, if we can watch this process, feel it happening, but respond in a calming way, this will result in those responses leaving our bodies.

Easier said than done, you might say. But by pausing at that moment and using our breathing to send calming messages back to the amygdala, we are stopping our thoughts from re-stimulating the fight or flight response in our brains. This is important when we consider our children's anxiety, as after that 90-second delay, we can influence how we respond to the fight or flight instinct.

Controlled breathing is scientifically proven to counter the stress response and is one of the most important tools we can teach our children to use so they can breathe through anxious moments. If our children practise controlled breathing, these deep, controlled breaths can slow the heart rate, lower blood pressure, and calm the fight or flight response set off by the amygdala.

·Ö· Top Tip!

For young children, I find the easiest way to explain the impact of controlled breathing is to tell them that when the amygdala, the little toddler, is worried that we might be in danger, it often checks in with us to see how we are responding. If we are taking long, calm breaths, it is as if he thinks to himself, 'Well, she doesn't seem too worried. If she thinks everything is OK, it can't be all that bad.' We are sending back a message of calm to him.

Controlled breathing is just breathing, right? Well, not exactly. Most of us don't really think about how we are breathing. We simply breathe. But if you stop for a moment and watch yourself breathing in a mirror, many of us, particularly if we are feeling anxious, will find that we are breathing into our upper lungs. You will probably see your upper chest expand and your shoulders move. This type of breathing is our go-to response when we are fearful. But we should aim to breathe down into our diaphragm, taking even, deep breaths, resulting in the air moving to our lower lungs. We usually call this *Belly Breathing* when speaking to children. This is the most efficient way to breathe. It starts in the nose and moves into the stomach as the diaphragm contracts and your lungs fill with air. Humans are naturally belly breathers. If you watch a young baby breathing, you will see them breathe down into their belly. By deliberately shifting our breathing in this way, we can stimulate the body's relaxation response, which is a calming influence.

So, how do we breathe like this?

- First, get comfortable. You can either stand or lie down.
- Place one hand on your chest and the other on your stomach.
- Start by taking a normal breath and exhale.
- Then, inhale slowly through your nose, taking the breath down into your stomach, allowing your chest and stomach to rise as you fill your lungs. You should feel the hand on your stomach rise.
- Pause for a moment, then breathe out slowly through your mouth, and repeat. These breaths should be slower and deeper than you usually take.
- Continue this breathing pattern for a few minutes, breathing gently into the lower lungs and expanding your abdomen. Let your breath flow as deep as is comfortable without forcing it.

You need to practise this calming breath on a regular basis. If you start practicing when lying down, move on to practicing it at other times during your day when standing. This controlled breathing encourages full oxygen exchange, slows the heartbeat, and can help stabilise blood pressure.

When you are teaching young children how to breathe in this way, ask them to start breathing in for a count of three, but encourage them to take a little longer on their out-breath. Breathing out for longer can move the nervous system away from the fight-or-flight mode towards rest-and-digest mode more effectively. As children become more experienced with this breathing, you can encourage the counts to become even longer. We usually say that your heartbeat will slow down, and you will feel a positive impact after about ten repetitions.

💡 Top Tip!

Breathing Buddies - a little stuffed cuddly toy or bean-filled toy - are a great way for children to practise controlled breathing. Children lie comfortably and place their breathing buddy on their stomachs. They then focus on the breathing buddy moving up and down as they slowly inhale and exhale. Doing this helps them to breathe down into their diaphragm. Get them to inhale through their nose for a count of three, down into their tummy until they see the breathing buddy move. Pause for a moment, then exhale for a count of four, pause for a moment, then repeat the process.

If your child struggles to focus, you can get him to silently say *in* to himself as he breathes in and *out* to himself as he breathes out. This can help younger children maintain a focus on the exercise. Another tip that works well for younger children is to practise breathing mantras when they practise their breathing. They can 'breathe in' a positive emotion and 'breathe out' a negative one. So, as they breathe in, they say to themselves, 'Breathe in calm,' and on the out-breath, they say 'Breathe out stress.' They can use any mantra that helps them breathe in the positive and breathe out the negative. For example: 'Breathe in bravery' and 'Breathe out worry' or 'Breathe in happiness' and 'Breathe out sadness.' Remind your child that this way of breathing sends the message back to their amygdala that all is well. It is also a way of showing your child that their breathing is within their control. Doing this exercise helps children calm down and focus. They begin to understand that paying attention to their breathing can help them relax when feeling anxious.

With older children, you might want to use a flat stone instead of a cuddly toy on their stomach. As with the breathing buddy, you ask them to focus on the stone moving up and down as they breathe.

Teenagers can also try the exercise standing up, with one hand placed on their chest and the other on their abdomen.

Whatever their age, if you get your children to practise this on a regular basis, every night before bed, and again as part of their regular daily routine, it becomes a learned behaviour. The more regularly your child practises this breathing, the more able they will become at putting it into practise when they need it.

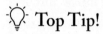 **Top Tip!**

If your child is feeling anxious, get them to stop what they are doing and close their eyes for a few minutes while they do their deep breathing. Closing their eyes helps to block out external stimuli and reset their calm brain.

Although there is no magic wand to wave away our children's anxiety, awareness of the 90-Second Rule and controlled breathing is important in terms of our ability to respond to stress. We know that this slow, deep breathing initiates the relaxation response that can neutralise the neurochemicals that cause the physical feeling of anxiety. However, this type of breathing will not come naturally to children, or even to adults, at times of anxiety. We need to practise, practise, practise it when calm. Encourage your child to make this a habit and practise it at the same time every day, maybe when they wake in the morning, after they come home from school, and before bedtime. Once they are familiar with it, they can be encouraged to use the technique when feeling stressed or anxious. Then, we can help support them in moving out of their comfort zones.

From the Horse's Mouth

I give online talks to secondary school students about anxiety. I can almost feel the eye rolls through the screen when I explain the difference that controlled breathing can make in their lives. If you have a child or teen who is not convinced that this breathing really works, explain that because it is an automatic response, they don't have to believe it will work. They just need to initiate it. I ask these teens to agree to practise their breathing every day, morning, and night, for a month. If it doesn't work, give it up. However, we know from science that it *will* work, so committing to trying it can give your teen time to see how effective it can be.

Practical Relaxation Tools

There are various other techniques you can use when encouraging relaxation in children who are struggling with anxiety or emotional regulation. A parent once told me she constantly told her young son to calm down before she realised he had no idea how to begin doing this. If we want our children to be calm or use a tool to cope when they are feeling stressed or anxious, we need to give them some age-appropriate tools to use. Here are a few ideas worth considering:

- **The Body Scan**

The squeeze and release *Body Scan* involves practicing tensing and relaxing different muscles in the body to induce calm. It also helps children recognise the difference between feeling tense and being relaxed.

Research conducted at Ulm University in Germany examined the impact of an 8-week Body Scan intervention on the stress levels of students[24]. They compared cortisol levels in students who listened to a

20-minute body scan nightly to those who listened to an audiobook. They found that the body scan group showed a decreased level of cortisol compared to the audiobook group. They concluded that daily mindful body scans can reduce biological and psychological stress.

For children who unconsciously hold tension in their bodies, taking the time to develop an awareness of this tension can help them not only create a sense of body awareness but also bring increased psychological wellbeing.

👍 Give it a Try!

Try a body scan yourself to see how it works.

Lie on your bed or the sofa and close your eyes. Start by taking a deep breath through your nose. Hold the breath for a moment, then breathe out through your mouth. Continue taking these deep breaths slowly while you are doing the body scan. Start by stretching out your legs, pointing your toes as far as they will stretch. Then, stretch out your arms at your sides, stretching to your fingertips. Now, we are going to start tensing all the muscles in our bodies, starting with our toes. Start to tense your toes, squeeze them as tightly as possible, then let the squeeze go. Then, begin to tense the muscles in your legs for a few moments. Again, squeeze as tightly as you can, then relax again. Next, tense your tummy up as tightly as you can, and then let go. Now, on to your arms. Squeeze them as tight as possible, clenching your fists, then relax. Move onto your shoulders and squeeze them tightly, then release. Now, try to tighten up all the muscles in your face, from the crinkles on your forehead to squeezing your lips together. As you relax, feel the softness in your forehead, and imagine your eyebrows sliding off the side of your face. Finally, let your whole body go limp again. Concentrate on your breath again. Breathe in slowly and deeply through your nose, hold for a moment, then release the breath through your mouth. As you release your breath, open your eyes and notice how relaxed your body is.

There are plenty of online tools which will direct you through a body scan with your child. One of my favourite mindfulness resources for children is the work of Louise Shanagher, children's therapist and founder of Creative Mindfulness Kids. Her *Mindfully Me* and *Kindfully Me* series of books are ones I often recommend to parents of little ones. She offers free Meditations for children on her website[25].

Ask the Expert

I spoke to Louise about the benefits of the body scan for children. She advises: 'The body scan is a fantastic exercise to support children in cultivating mindfulness of the body, emotions, and physical sensations. The body scan supports children to notice what it feels like inside their bodies. Another word for this is interoception. Scientists have shown that cultivating sensitivity to our internal sensations can support children's ability to regulate emotions as well as reduce feelings of anxiety and depression. Body scan meditations help children focus their attention on the present moment. When children focus on sensations in their bodies, this supports them in letting thoughts and worries go and become more connected to the here and now. When practiced on a regular basis, the body scan meditation supports children in increasing their focus and concentration and being better able to manage difficult thoughts and worries.

Body scan practises can support children to identify where they might be holding tension in their bodies and learn how to relax that tension. As children release tension in their bodies, this will help them feel calmer and reduce anxiety. The mind and body are inextricably linked. As the body rests and relaxes, the mind will also begin to rest and relax. The body scan can be a very soothing experience for children. It can help activate their parasympathetic nervous system and support them in falling asleep.'

With practise, this method helps the child be aware of their body and the tension contained within it. So often, parents and teachers will say that children fell asleep the first time they tried it. After the scan, you can talk to them about how it felt to tense up and how it felt to release. Finally, ask them, now that they have gone through the exercise, if their body feels more tense or more relaxed. The idea is that they start to recognise the sensations within their body and how strong emotions can impact them in physical ways.

- **Glitter Jars**

Glitter jars were developed initially for children who struggle with self-regulation but can be equally useful for children dealing with anxiety or any stressful situation. A glitter jar is a glass jar filled with water, clear glue, and glitter. If angry or upset, the child shakes the jar, and the glitter swirls, representing their feelings. Then they sit and relax while doing their belly breathing and watch the glitter as it swirls until it settles on the bottom of the jar. The glitter represents everything going on inside their heads, inside their hearts, and inside their bodies. As they breathe slowly, the glitter settles just like their feelings.

☙ Give it a Try!

To make a glitter jar at home, clean off the outside of the jar and ask the child to choose coloured glitter to place in the jar. They can choose colours to represent their emotions – red for anger, green for jealousy, purple for anxiety and so on. They can also add larger sequins to represent the things they have in life to ground them. For example, a sequin could represent a parent, a grandparent, or even a pet. These larger sequins will settle to the bottom more quickly than the smaller glitter pieces and remind the child of the good things they have in their life as they breathe. Remember to add the clear glue when making the jar, as it helps with the swirling motion. Also, use hot water when making the jar initially. It is a good idea to glue the lid back onto the jar to avoid leaks. There are plenty of online tutorials to talk you through the process step by step.

I cannot stress enough the benefits of these jars. The glitter is such a concrete representation of what the child is feeling. Watching the glitter settle as they breathe deeply is a positive strategy for the child to use when they want to address their anxiety or, indeed, any strong emotion.

From the Horse's Mouth

A student of mine told me about a particular boy in her preschool class who she felt would really benefit from a glitter jar. She made the jars in class and demonstrated to the children how to use them. As expected, this boy was using his jar quite often. She would see him glaring at his friend if they argued, then march over to his glitter jar on the shelf, glaring back at his friend the whole way. Then, sometimes, she would see his friend glare back and then march over to his glitter jar. She said it was like 'Gunfight at the O.K. Corral' in the beginning, with these two four-year-olds having a stand-off, both furiously shaking their glitter jars at each other! But soon, they learned the benefit of breathing out their anger and frustration, and the glitter jars did their work.

• Worry Time

Another useful tool is to create a worry box for children to put their worries in or to create a daily ritual of *Worry Time* with your child when they talk about their worries. You can do this every day, maybe more than once a day at the beginning, but over time, you may not need to do it as often.

I usually recommend that worry time take place when the child comes in from school (after they have been fed and watered) and again in the evening. Try not to do it last thing at night. If you want to do it as part of the bedtime routine, do it before bath and story time. Then, after those times, leave your body scan or controlled breathing exercises till last thing at night.

During worry time, encourage your children to release all their worries. You can write them down, or your child can draw them and put them into a worry box, or you can just talk about them, depending on the age and preference of the child. Young children often like to make a worry box that they can decorate themselves. Older children might prefer to write worries on Post-it notes and put them in a worry jar or write them in a journal. During worry time, anything, no matter how small it seems, constitutes a valid worry.

However, worry time is limited. The idea is to stop the child from spending the whole day ruminating over their worries but to get them used to the idea of focusing on them for a short while instead. It may be a 10, 15 or 20-minute period, but when the time is up, close the box and say goodbye to the worries for the day. Just remember your job is not to 'fix' these worries. This is not a time for debate or giving advice (unless specifically asked). It is a time to really listen to your child's worries.

Say you have worry time with your child after they have come in from school. You talk through their worries and maybe write them down and put them in their worry box. Then, later, you are making dinner, and your child comes running up with worries they had forgotten to tell you about earlier in the day. You want to try to stop the whole evening from becoming worry time, but you also don't want to dismiss the child's worries. So, you can say, 'Oh, it sounds as if that was hard for you. I really want to hear all about that. Will you make sure you save that one and tell me all about it at worry time?' You can then focus on doing something else with the child. The child knows you are acknowledging the worry, but you want to focus on something else now. Just one proviso: if your child comes in later in the day and something has happened to upset them, of course, you will not put them off. You are only trying to pause the worries from earlier in the day. If they have an upset at any given moment, you will, of course, be empathetic to their needs.

Postponing talking about their worries can sound a little bit harsh to start with, but if you have a child who tends to dwell on their worries all day long, it is so much better for them to slowly get used to limiting the time they spend in this way. The aim is to reduce the time spent on worry time, and perhaps move it to once a day. You are not dismissing their worries but empowering the child by teaching them that they can postpone some of their worries until later.

☼ Top Tip!

If the child finds they are dwelling on their worries all day in school, you can ask them to imagine they are putting the worry into a worry box in their mind. This allows them to save it for worry time at home while they are freed up to do something else in school. It can be hard to wait for worry time, but after a while, they will find they can't remember all the little worries of the day.

Encourage older children to write down their worries during worry time. Taking the time to write helps to slow down their overthinking brain. Seeing their concerns on paper also gives some perspective.

Some children like to store their worries in a worry box. If this helps 'park' their fears, it is worth doing, but try not to let them store the worries without talking to you about them. Taking the time to talk through their worries shows you acknowledge the importance of these thoughts and can open discussions about possible faulty thinking.

At the end of worry time, when their worries have been talked about, maybe written down, and placed in a worry box or jar, it can be good to shift the focus. To do this, at the end of worry time, I recommend briefly making a note or thinking about three things your child was grateful for that day. It might be their teacher, chatting with Grandad, or spending time playing with their dog, anything that reminds them of the good things in their life.

- **Sensory Objects**

The sense of touch can also be a powerful tool to help us calm down. Children's hands and fingers can be a source of soothing, so physical objects that they touch can help them to self-regulate.

🦉 A Word to the Wise

Have you ever wondered why a paper cut can hurt so much? It's all to do with anatomy. Logically, a tiny cut on your finger should not hurt as much as a larger cut on another part of your body. However, our fingertips have more nerve endings than any other part of the body. Fingertips are important tools with which we explore the world, so it makes sense that we have a lot of nerve endings and pain receptors there as a safety mechanism. So, although paper cuts are tiny, they are in a very sensitive area where the brain magnifies sensation.

Sensory objects are items we slowly touch that help the brain to calm. These can be objects like smooth stones to rub in your hands, fabrics of different textures to slowly feel, buttons with raised surfaces, or fidget spinners, all of which can help children to self-soothe. Engaging with sensory materials like finger paints, Play-Doh, stretchy materials like slime or Blu Tack, or even water play can help calm a child. Some children find the sensation of a cold compress calming or dipping their hands in water therapeutic.

• A Coping Toolbox

A *Coping Toolbox* is a box filled with practical coping strategies that will help a child to calm, self-regulate, and express their emotions in a positive way. The toolbox usually contains items that help the child cope in various ways and focus on different senses. For example:

- For sounds, perhaps an audio of some nature sounds, wind chimes, or a singing bowl. You might also include noise-cancelling head-phones for children who need relief from sounds.
- For sight, some photos of loved ones or pets, maybe photos of holidays past or favourite places. You could also include colouring books or paint sets.
- For smell, perhaps some essential oils or a favourite scented candle. Maybe Dad's aftershave or Mum's perfume or body lotion. Smells that register safety. You might even include some herbs or spices.
- For touch, some swatches of soft material or cuddly toys. A stress ball, a fidget spinner, or even some bubble wrap for popping. You could also include a weighted blanket, which can be a very effective sleep aid for children by providing a sense of safety and security in bed.

- For taste, some of the child's favourite flavours. Mints, chewing gum, flavoured waters, or sweets. Perhaps squares of chocolate for the child to melt in their mouth.

The strategies for stress relief will be personal to each child and should not only include items linked to the senses as outlined above but also more general objects. Your child might like to include written affirmations or items that encourage physical movement, such as a skipping rope or resistance bands. Additionally, you could include items like bubbles for blowing, mindfulness cards with inspirational messages, or arts and crafts activities.

Give it a Try!

Help your child make a coping toolbox. They need a box with a lid, like an old gift box or shoebox. They can wrap and decorate the box as they like. Then, fill the box with items such as photos of friends and family, souvenirs from past holidays, photos or drawings of their pets, certificates of achievement, sports medals, and anything else that reminds the child that they are loved, valued, strong and capable. You can also add sensory objects as described above so they are at hand when needed. Leave the box in plain view to remind the child that the contents are ready and available when needed.

An Attitude of Gratitude

Taking time to enjoy our world is important not only for our children who struggle with anxiety but for all of us. In our modern world, we spend so much time rushing from activity to activity, from work to home, and from place to place. How often do we take the time to stop and enjoy our world and appreciate the good within our lives? Research shows that taking time to enjoy a pleasant scene in nature or in your mind for up to ten seconds three times a day can help to rewire your brain to focus on the positive.

American Psychologist Robert Emmons is the world's leading scientific expert on gratitude. Having researched this area for over a decade, he studied the impact of gratitude on physical and psychological health and wellbeing. He found that simple gratitude practices adopted daily for as little as three weeks result in a host of benefits. From physical benefits such as improved immune systems, better sleep, and lower blood pressure to psychological benefits such as reporting a more positive outlook on life and greater levels of optimism and happiness. Studies also found these practices make people feel more compassionate, helpful, and forgiving. Emmons defines gratitude as having two components. Firstly, a belief that there is good in our lives and in the world around us. Secondly, a vision of where that goodness comes from, both within us and from within others. He argues that gratitude makes us appreciate the value of little positives in our world that we might otherwise take for granted.

To encourage an attitude of gratitude within our children, we can set aside time every day to remind ourselves of the good things in our world. If our children keep a gratitude journal and each evening write down three things from their day they are thankful for, this encourages them to consider the good in their lives. Little ones can draw three things or talk about them rather than write them down. These things can be moments within their day they are grateful for, people or pets who make their lives better. Anything within their lives they are thankful for. Doing this every day will focus our children intentionally on developing a more grateful approach to life and guard against taking things for granted.

An alternative approach, as a family, is to practise gratitude together. You can do this with a gratitude jar. Each family member writes down something they are grateful for every day or so, and at the end of the month, you open the jar and read out all the things you are thankful for as a family.

We also know that writing down our thoughts, fears, and worries can help us to gain clarity. Journalling has been recognised as a tool for supporting wellbeing by helping children process their anxious thoughts by putting them down on paper, which can help take a weight off their shoulders — in essence, leaving the worry on the page. Encouraging your child or teen to write down their worries and thoughts while expressing both positive and more tricky emotions provides a safe space for them to express themselves freely. It can help your child to understand their thoughts and emotions better while reflecting on any worries they may have.

👍 Give it a Try!

Here are some journalling prompts you can give your children to focus on as they develop the skill of writing their thoughts:

- Write about something you would like to do when you are older.
- Write about your favourite memory.
- Write about what makes a good friend.
- Write about a challenge you faced and what you did to cope.
- Write about three things that make you feel happy.
- Write about someone you admire.
- Write about your favourite superhero power.
- Write about three things you are proud of.
- Write about something you would like to learn more about.
- Write about your favourite hobby, book, or TV show.
- Write a message to little you.

Journal prompts like the above examples can make the process easier, particularly as they get used to the idea of expressing their thoughts. Having a topic to write about can help with inspiration. You can also use a personal prompt to direct them toward a topic you would like them to explore further to understand their thoughts and feelings better. As they become more familiar with journalling, they will no longer need prompts.

 ## From the Horse's Mouth

If you feel your child would be better able to start trying to journal in a more structured way, there are plenty of journals for children and teens that take a more structured form. Here are a few worth considering:

- My Mind Really Matters (6-12 years and 12+ versions)
- The Big Life Journal (6-12 years and 12+ versions)
- The Happy Self Kids Daily Journal (6-12 years and 12+ versions)
- The Positive Doodle Diary (6-10 years)

These all contain inspirational quotes, fun facts, and uplifting mantras and exercises to support wellbeing.

Developing an attitude of gratitude can help our children develop a more optimistic outlook on life, something that those who struggle with anxiety can most definitely benefit from. It can help them take a more positive approach to life and show more compassion not only to others but, most importantly, towards themselves. It can also help a child to shift their internal focus from themselves to an appreciation of others. Cultivating this attitude helps a child focus on the positives rather than dwell on their worries.

The Power of Habit

To finish this chapter, remember the importance of habit forming. You may have seen self-help advice state that it takes twenty-one days to develop a habit. Modern science doesn't back up this statistic. It takes longer. So, if you find that it is taking time for your child to settle into a routine of mindfulness practices, I encourage you to give it some time. Once a new behaviour becomes a routine, it takes less discipline to maintain.

We know from psychology that we best focus on adopting one good habit at a time. Don't try to take on lots of new mindfulness practices in your life together. Focus on one significant aspect and develop that skill. Once that is firmly established, build on it. University College London conducted a research project examining how long it can take for a new behaviour to become so ingrained that we would consider it to have become automatic. They found that it takes, on average, sixty-six days to acquire a new habit. Don't let this put you off, as further research suggests that once we have spent time acquiring a new habit, the halo effect takes place, whereby not only the first behaviour becomes easier, but we are more likely to find other positive habits easier to adopt as well. So, if we can sustain the discipline long enough to develop one good habit, others are likely to follow.

The concept of habit stacking may also help. Habit stacking is a proven formula whereby you attach a new habit to an already-formed habit. For example, if you are practicing belly breathing with your child each morning before school, pair it with another activity. Do it immediately after breakfast. Or every evening immediately after their bedtime story. Essentially, your brain links the two behaviours, expecting one habit to follow the other. Start by looking at the habits your child already has in their day to find a solid habit to anchor from. Perhaps they attend sports activities every Tuesday and Thursday evening, come home, and have a bath. Well, start doing a Body Scan immediately after their bath. Maybe leave their Glitter Jar on the desk where they do their homework so it is right in view when they are likely to need it most. As the neurological wiring in your brain is already in place for the first habit, which you most likely perform on autopilot, it is easier to piggyback a second habit onto that task.

From the Horse's Mouth

If you struggle with bringing in new habits for your children, remember we all tend towards the easiest path—the path we are used to treading. I walk with friends a few mornings a week at the Hill of Tara. We automatically follow the same path every day we walk. That pathway has become embedded in our brains as the route to follow. Occasionally, we change our route, and the place we know like the back of our hands, now feels unfamiliar. We notice things we have never noticed and see the Hill from a new perspective, yet we are always drawn back to that same old familiar route. Similarly, the neural pathways in our children's brains are wired to follow the most well-used route. The longer they have been following those well-worn pathways of response to their anxiety, the more embedded those actions have become. Changing the pathways in their brains involves changing their automatic responses to challenging situations. It involves more effort to take a new pathway. But if we can support them over time to embed these new habits into their day, by a process of repetition, they will form new neural pathways in their brains, with healthier responses to anxious thoughts.

If anxiety is deeply entrenched, your child will need to practise the skills outlined in this book for some time before they see positive change. As they start to make changes, it can cause discomfort, and they may try to avoid making any changes. Try to remember that you are giving them the tools to help them face future challenges, even though changing well-worn patterns can take some time. The skills they are developing, which help them self-regulate and find their inner calm, are the foundations they need when we go on to support them to face their fears.

CHAPTER 5

Facing Fears and Changing Patterns

When our kids struggle with their mental health
We need to lean in, not step back.
We need to be the anchors,
and hold them steady through stormy seas.

Dr Katie Hurley[26]

Now that we have ideas in place for self-regulation and support that we can use to help our children calm when anxiety hits, the next step is to look at how we can gently ease them out of their comfort zones. We can do this with trust and connection, remembering that the biggest influence we have is their relationship with us. We know the importance of one good adult, so let's look at how we can take an active role in helping to manage their anxiety.

Build a Fear Ladder

Avoidance is the go-to response for many children to their anxiety, and one of our goals as parents should be to help them avoid avoidance. The *Step Ladder* approach and the *Imagined Edge* are two particularly useful techniques in supporting our children to move out of their comfort zones slowly. Both approaches stem from the idea of gradual exposure, which means facing your fears step-by-step. Rather than avoiding situations which make your child anxious or advising them to jump in the deep end and risk the child becoming completely overwhelmed, these techniques involve starting with a situation that provokes the least amount of anxiety and slowly moving towards more challenging situations. It is basically a step-by-step approach to climbing the ladder of anxiety, breaking the task into manageable pieces, and using gradual exposure to reach a goal.

• The Step Ladder

Before you start, you need to talk to the child about the process and how it works. Along with your child, you picture a simple step ladder with several rungs. Together, you decide on the final goal, and this task becomes the top of the ladder. The first step becomes the starting point - ideally, a situation which causes your child the least anxiety. Together, you agree on the individual small steps to take to reach the goal, with each one a little more challenging than the previous step. It is very important that the child is an active partner in this process.

With little ones, they can draw a step ladder, so they have a tangible image to work with. You can then either write down the goal on each step of the ladder or let the child draw a picture of that goal. Having a concrete representation of the ladder is very helpful for younger children.

It is important that the tasks on each step of the ladder are not too daunting. The idea is that although the child is facing a greater challenge with each step, these are manageable and will result in them developing more confidence as they slowly proceed through each step. Anxiety will drop over time as you go through the laddering process. It might not drop to zero. It will take time. But the process can really help a child to manage their anxiety and get over their fears.

Before the child takes the first step, talk about the strategies they have been practicing for managing their anxiety, such as controlled breathing. Remind your child of the skill sets they now have so they know what to do as soon as they start to feel anxious. The goal is to encourage your child to sit with their anxiety at every step on the ladder until their anxiety has subsided. The child will feel uncomfortable, but by staying in the situation, they are confirming they are brave enough to handle it.

☝ Give it a Try!

Here is an example of the Step Ladder for a little girl who has separation anxiety and does not want her mother to be out of her sight.

Step 1: She plays in her room while Mum sits and reads in the corner.

Step 2: She plays in her room while Mum is in the adjoining room.

Step 3: She plays in her room while Mum cleans the bathroom.

Step 4: She plays in her room while Mum is downstairs.

Step 5: She plays in the house while Mum puts the washing on the line.

Step 6: She stays home with Dad while Mum nips to the shop.

Step 7: She stays home with Dad while Mum goes out for lunch.

Step 8: She says home with Granny while Mum and Dad go to lunch.

Step 9: Granny babysits while Mum and Dad go out for the evening.

Step 10: Granny babysits for the day while Mum and Dad go out.

Step 11: She goes to a friend's house to play for an hour.
Step 12: She goes to a friend's house to play for the afternoon.

Some steps might prove more challenging than others and need a longer time span to achieve. Most steps will need to be practised for some time before they become manageable. But as a parent, it is important that you recognise that each step, no matter how small, represents an achievement.

We know that anxious feelings don't last forever. Our bodies will only maintain high levels of anxiety for a short time. The laddering technique ensures that the child is not completely overwhelmed but takes small, gradual steps to overcome anxiety.

It is important not to rush the process. Too much fear will result in *flooding*, an emotionally overwhelming response where the child ends up completely flooded with anxiety. This can be very distressing and result in them feeling more traumatised. It may take some time for the child to feel ready to progress through each step. Don't force the pace. Instead, encourage them. You want them to feel a sense of mastery as they accomplish a step. Don't worry if progress is slow. Remember, each step is a step in the right direction.

The best way to deal with anxiety is not to try to remove all the stressors that cause it. Instead, it is to support the child to function as well as they can in the anxiety-provoking situation. If a child is very gradually exposed to anxiety-provoking situations, over time, their anxiety diminishes. When the child is initially exposed to the anxiety-provoking experience, their anxiety rises rapidly. However, if we can support the child to slowly sit with the anxiety, it will decrease in severity. Move at the speed of trust. Offer lots of praise and remind them they are showing bravery each time they achieve another step on the ladder.

Facing these fears shows the child they can cope with more than they previously believed possible. They also come to understand that the breathing techniques they have learned can help them cope with stressful situations. Finally, they gain a real sense of achievement as they progress up the ladder and face their fears.

👍 Give it a Try!

Here is another example of a Step Ladder. This time, for a child who was barked at by a large dog in the park and now has a fear of dogs.

Step 1: Look at pictures of dogs.

Step 2: Watch a film with a dog as the main character.

Step 3: Drive to the park and watch dogs from the car window.

Step 4: A friend visits with their small, friendly dog, and the child watches from the window.

Step 5: A friend visits with their dog, and the child watches from a distance in the garden.

Step 6: A friend holds their dog while the child stands close but does not touch it.

Step 7: A friend holds their dog while the child is encouraged to pet him.

Step 8: Stay in the garden while the dog runs around.

Step 9: Pick up and hold the dog.

Step 10: Go for a walk in a park where dogs are on leashes.

Step 11: Go for a walk in a park where dogs run free.

As they progress through the laddering process, take a bit of time to talk to your child about all they have achieved. It can be useful to consider their experiences of the process and what they have learned from it.

Here are some questions that should give you some ideas for discussion with your child about the laddering process and what they have learned about themselves as they have completed it:

- Looking back now, was facing that fear more difficult or easier than you expected?
- Before you started the process, would you have believed that you could face those challenges and cope with how they made you feel?
- What did you learn about how you could hope with things that make you feel anxious?
- Can you think of any other situations where you could use what you have learned in this process?

As you have these conversations, remind them about how brave they have been, how they have the courage to face something that was causing them such anxiety, and how this has changed them.

From the Horse's Mouth

I must briefly address one issue here that is important to note. The above idea is based on the notion of graded exposure to the experiences that are causing anxiety. The advice above will work for most children. We have taught them the self-regulation skills they need, and now we are slowly, step by step, exposing them to situations that make them anxious. However, sometimes, the fundamental cause of the anxiety needs to be addressed before you can use this system. We spoke earlier about the idea that the amygdala cannot tell the difference between the house burning down and burnt toast. This is important to consider because, in some cases, the house really is burning down. This is not a case of burnt toast. Take school anxiety as an example. Perhaps your child is being bullied in school, so she does not feel psychologically safe in that environment. Perhaps your child is neurodivergent and has sensory issues, and the noises or smells of the classroom are overwhelming them. Perhaps your child has a learning difficulty which is not being supported in school. In these cases, the amygdala is right - the house really is burning down. The underlying issues will not be resolved by greater exposure. In fact, it may make them worse. Bullying, sensory issues, and so on are underlying problems that need to be considered, either through engagement with the school or with professional support before you can deal with the anxiety.

• The Imagined Edge

Similar to the *Step Ladder* approach is an even gentler approach called *Think It, Feel It, Do It* involving the *Imagined Edge*. This technique is outlined by Lawrence Cohen in his book, *The Opposite of Worry*[27]. Cohen starts by outlining the *Fear-O-Meter*, a scale from 0-10, which you can use with your child to rank intensity levels of distress. The scale should be individual to the child and represent how low or high their anxiety levels feel. Parents should agree on the wording of this scale with their child. For example, 0 might represent a piece of cake, 5 might represent getting tough, and 10 might represent about to explode with anxiety. Once the scale is agreed (and for younger children, once again, drawing a picture of the scale can be a good idea), you ask the child, 'What is your number right now?' The child identifies where they are on the scale at that point in time. This scale is also a useful way to measure the effectiveness of any anti-anxiety technique by asking the child what their number is before and after using their controlled breathing, for example.

💡 Top Tip!

For younger children, a scale from 1-5 might be more helpful. Something like:

- 1: Feeling calm and relaxed.
- 2: Feeling a little worried.
- 3: Feeling nervous.
- 4: Feeling very anxious.
- 5: Feeling out of control.

The idea is that the child vividly imagines the step which causes them anxiety (Think It). This pushes them to experience the same anxiety as if they were facing it in real life (Feel It). After repeatedly doing this, they are ready to face the task in real life (Do It).

As with the Step Ladder approach, parent and child agree on a hierarchy of situations which cause anxiety. The child starts to vividly imagine the lowest-level situation, and the parent asks, 'What is your number right now?' At that point, the child might be at a 7. They then do their controlled breathing (or another anxiety-lowering technique if preferred). After a while, the parent asks for their number, which would be expected to be lower down the scale. The process is repeated over and over, with the child moving up and down the scale, but with each repetition, their anxiety about that specific thought is lowered.

Using an example of a child who cannot bring themselves to go to school, the first step might be to imagine getting up in the morning and putting on their school uniform. The next step might be to imagine packing their schoolbag with their lunch and water bottle and leaving the house for school. The next step might be to imagine driving to school, standing in the yard, and so on. When each level stops raising the number on the Fear-O-Meter, your child is ready to try imagining the next step on the hierarchy. Over time, this process will support the child in facing their anxiety and seeing they have tools to enable them to cope in stressful situations.

If you remember the neural connections I mentioned earlier, this process can have an impact on them. We know the amygdala cannot tell the difference between real danger and perceived danger. It responds the same way to these imagined situations as it would to the real-life experience. If you are anything like me with a fear of heights, you may already know this. As someone with this fear, if I watch a video of someone up at a height, my body physically responds exactly as it would if I were up at the height myself. Even imagining these situations can provoke the same responses. By doing these exercises, we are setting up the neural pathways to adapt to these anxiety-provoking situations. It is important to tell the child that every time they think these brave thoughts and face their fears, they are strengthening the areas of the brain that will help them ride the wave of anxiety.

CBT and Cognitive Distortions

Cognitive Behavioural Therapy (CBT) is based on the concept that how we think impacts how we feel, which in turn impacts how we act. So, anxiety causes our children to have persistent negative thoughts, which lead to destructive behaviour patterns. Through this lens, it is the meaning we give to events, the way in which we interpret them, that gives rise to feelings of anxiety. The idea is that anxiety is made up of three things. Thoughts – these are the thoughts our children have internally. Feelings – this is how their body reacts to those thoughts. Behaviours – this is how they respond to those feelings, their actions.

Here are three examples of how thoughts might impact feelings which impact on behaviour:

- *Thought*: The teacher said she would check students' reading tomorrow.
- *Feeling*: Scared to read in class, so a stomach-ache develops.
- *Behaviour*: Avoid school in case I throw up.

- *Thought*: What if someone breaks into our house?
- *Feeling*: Apprehension, frightened to be alone in bed.
- *Behaviour*: Need to sleep in with Mum and Dad.

- *Thought*: What if Mum gets killed in a car accident?
- *Feeling*: Fearful and worried.
- *Behaviour*: Do not want mum to leave the house or be separated from her.

In terms of supporting our children, the message is that if children have learned unhelpful thoughts, feelings, and behaviours, they can also be unlearned. A CBT therapist works with the child, highlighting their negative thoughts and behaviour patterns, then challenges these patterns, enabling the child to become more logical in their thinking. Once your child can identify these thoughts, they can learn to tolerate them. Tolerating the thought involves learning that it is OK to have fearful thoughts that may make you uncomfortable, but by challenging them, you can withstand these scary thoughts.

CBT has been proven to be very effective when working with children with phobias, panic attacks, and generalised anxiety disorder. Psychiatrist Dr Aaron Beck from the University of Pennsylvania is known as the father of Cognitive Behavioural Therapy. The Beck Institute reports that CBT has been scientifically tested and found to be effective in more than 2,000 studies for the treatment of various mental health conditions. They advise that, when implemented correctly, CBT helps individuals get better and stay better.

As part of his work on CBT, Aaron Beck identified several illogical patterns of thinking that he calls *thought distortions*, which he suggested cause anxiety. These ways of thinking involve assumptions which often misrepresent reality and can promote negativity. These include:

- *Magnification*: exaggerating the importance of a negative event.
- *Minimisation*: underplaying the significance of a positive event.
- *Personalisation*: blaming yourself for an event or situation you were not responsible for.
- *Overgeneralisation*: coming to negative conclusions about future failure based on a single negative experience.
- *Arbitrary Interference*: often called mind reading, which means drawing negative conclusions based on limited evidence.
- *Selective Abstraction*: focusing on a negative aspect of a situation while ignoring the positive – measuring yourself by perceived failures.

These cognitive distortions come from our tendency as humans to make associations between two variables, believing that one has caused the other when there is no proof.

Following on from Beck's work, many other cognitive distortions have been identified. Some of the most common cognitive distortions our children may experience are *Ruminating* (going over the same thoughts again and again) and *Catastrophising* (thinking about the worst things that could happen). These two often go together, where a child will keep revisiting the same thought, each time coming up with a worse conclusion. Many children with cognitive distortions also tend to engage in *All or Nothing Thinking*, where they view the world in black or white terms, with very little nuance in between. They class situations and people as being either good or bad.

We know that humans often fall into the trap of making causal associations between things that happen in sequence. We assume that the first thing caused the other. This is not surprising as, from babies, we are hard-wired to look for patterns and develop theories on why these are happening. It is human nature to interpret the world around us and try to process each experience in a way that makes sense to us. This sometimes involves our brain taking 'shortcuts' and coming to erroneous conclusions. From worrying that your partner has been involved in a car crash when they are late home from work one evening to thinking we have offended a friend who was just stressed about her own life to focusing on answers that suit our own personal biases. We all do it. But the important thing is to make sure we challenge these thoughts if they are becoming our go-to way of thinking.

Sometimes, we need to stand back and properly review the evidence to see if the conclusions we are jumping to are correct. In the case of our children, cognitive distortions make them feel worse about themselves and the situations they find themselves in. They also allow their behaviour to be directed by these thoughts.

Psychologist Martin Seligman argues that, linked to the above, anxious teens tend to engage in three cognitive distortions that increase anxiety. They personalise situations, making it all about them. For example, 'It is my fault that this person doesn't want to be my friend.' They assume permanence, so they assume that things will not change, but the negativity they feel will always be present. And they make things pervasive, so not only will that person not want to be their friend, but no one will.

You can use *reframing* to help your child see alternative explanations for managing anxious thoughts. By showing curiosity about what a child is feeling, we can facilitate a reframing conversation, helping them to see their problems in a new light. Asking open-ended questions is one way we can do this. Instead of telling your child what you think they are feeling or offering reassurance, you are checking in with their emotions. You can do this by describing what you see and investigating their understanding of it. By saying something like, 'Oh, pet, you look pretty upset about school today. I am curious to try to understand what you are feeling. Can you tell me more about what happened?' You are opening the discussion by telling the child that you are curious about their feelings and would like to understand them better. As they explain their emotions, it can help you to see any cognitive distortions within their thinking. You are trying to help them analyse the way they look at challenging situations and help them come up with healthier ways to approach them.

☝ Give it a Try:

Some questions that can be useful to discuss with children when working through challenging situations are:

- What would you say to your friend if she was going through this situation?
- If [person they admire] was here, what advice do you think they might give?
- If you could change one thing about this situation, what would you change?
- Can you think of any time you have faced something similar in the past?

The THINK acronym is often used when speaking to children and teens about how they communicate with others both face-to-face and via information they post online. THINK reminds a child to consider the language they use when interacting with others. They ask themselves, before they speak or post online, if it is True, Helpful, Inspiring, Necessary, or Kind? We can also use this acronym to help them consider their own thoughts and how they respond to themselves. Firstly, is this thought True? It is important to separate facts from fiction when considering our thoughts. If the thought is an opinion rather than a fact, then maybe we need to challenge it. Secondly, is it Helpful? Is this thought useful to me or others? If not, it is time to either ignore or challenge it. Thirdly, is it Inspiring? If this thought doesn't inspire me, maybe I should ignore it. Fourthly, is it Necessary?

If it is not necessary to focus on this thought or to act on it at this moment, then maybe I should let it go. Finally, is it Kind? If this thought is not kind to me or to others, if this thought is hurting me or could hurt anyone else, I should not give it any of my time.

Using the THINK acronym can help our children take back control of their thoughts and make better decisions about which thoughts to consider and which to ignore. Pressing their inner pause button while they consider their thoughts using the acronym also gives them a little space to distance themselves from the emotion the thought brings up. A moment to pause and reflect on the thought can take some of the power out of it.

We can also help our children re-frame negative thoughts by encouraging them to be thought detectives. They can do this by considering the evidence available to support that thought. You can ask your child to explain their faulty thought to you and how that thought made them feel. Then, consider how that thought and feeling impacted their behaviour. After that, ask them if they can think of any proof that the thought was true or if it is possible that it was a faulty thought. Considering the evidence for the thought and the evidence against it can help our children move from the negative towards the positive and re-frame the thought to a more realistic one.

Supporting your child to question their anxious thoughts is a great way to help them gather evidence to support or disprove them. Start by asking them if the event they fear has ever happened in the past. If so, when did it last happen? How many times has it happened? If it happened, how bad was it? The aim is to help them understand that by examining the evidence gained by these questions, you can think about the likelihood of these feared events happening and develop a more realistic understanding. However, we must remember that anxious brains take time to change, so it is only by repeatedly challenging their thoughts that progress is made.

It is also important not only to challenge these thoughts but also to develop coping thoughts. Asking these evidence-based questions can also help build constructive thinking about challenging situations. So, if we consider the example given above:

- *Thought*: What if Mum gets killed in a car accident?
- *Feeling*: Fearful and worried
- *Behaviour*: Do not want Mum to leave the house

By challenging these thoughts, we can help the child see that Mum has never been in an accident. However, she has previously come home late. The time she came home late, she had gotten distracted at work, nothing serious happened, and we all coped. The most likely explanation if she is late again, is that she is distracted at work. If Mum is late getting home again, we can use this as a coping thought.

Give It a Try!

Questioning the negative thoughts that determine anxious feelings can also be helpful. It helps a child to see that a negative thought is not always true. Here are a few questions you might use to help you challenge your child's tricky thoughts:

- Is this thought helpful? Does it improve the situation in any way?
- Is this thought a fact? Can I think of any evidence to support that this thought is fact? Or have I confused a thought with a fact?
- Is this thought focusing only on the negative? Is there a more positive alternative to this thought?
- How important will this thought be next month or next year?
- Is there something I can do to change this situation? Can I think of any possible solutions?
- Am I expecting myself to be perfect?

We can all focus on the negative at times, and sometimes, we must stop and re-focus in a more positive or self-accepting way. Our thoughts impact very strongly on our feelings and on to our behaviour. Accepting these negative thoughts as facts has implications on how we act based on these faulty assumptions. If they become a learned behaviour, these cognitive distortions can become completely entrenched and cloud rational thinking. For children caught in a cycle of negative thinking, professional support in re-framing can help break these thought patterns and enable them to live in a more self-accepting way. Engaging with a qualified CBT therapist can also be helpful to support children or teens with very entrenched cognitive distortions.

The Science of Sleep and Rest

We know that every biological process in the human body improves with sleep. Consistent good sleep is very important for our wellbeing. Indeed, poor sleeping patterns have been shown to impact mental health. But to get to sleep, some complex processes need to occur. We need melatonin and sleep pressure. Sleep pressure (the need to sleep) can be impacted by cortisol. As mentioned previously, this is a chemical produced in the body when we feel anxious, which makes it harder for children struggling with anxiety to fall asleep.

There are five main stages of the sleep cycle. The first four are called NREM (non-rapid eye movement). This type of sleep is important for wellbeing and memory. The final one is REM (rapid eye movement), which is important for processing information and memories from the day. It takes approximately 90 to 120 minutes to go through a complete cycle of these stages, so a child who is sleeping well will go through these stages four or five times each night. The final cycle is argued to be the most restorative than the earlier phases.

We know that up to 50% of children will experience a sleep problem at some stage in their childhood. But for many children who struggle with anxiety, sleep can be an ongoing issue. Anxieties under the surface during the day may come to the fore at bedtime when there are no distractions to keep them at bay.

Before you even consider trying to encourage the child to sleep, it can help to start with some form of connection. You are bringing the focus back to connection with you, rather than separation from you to sleep. If you have quality time with your child before you start the sleep routine, giving your child undivided attention, you provide them with the time and space to talk about any worries they may have in a relaxed way before the separation of sleep.

Give it a Try!

The three-question technique is an effective way to check in with your child before bedtime. Before winding down for bed, ask them the following three questions:

- Tell me about something that went well today.
- Tell me about something a little tricky today.
- Is there anything else you would like me to know about today?

If a child has trouble thinking of things to tell you, start by sharing your responses to the questions with them. Doing this eases the transition to bedtime. It brings the focus back to their connection with you.

Being worried at bedtime can trigger the fight or flight response, and that is most definitely not conducive to a good night's sleep. Children with anxiety at bedtime may struggle to fall asleep, lie awake for hours, and then maybe wake up during the night. They often find every excuse under the sun to get Mum or Dad back into the bedroom with them. They are too hot or too cold. It is too dark or too bright.

They are hungry, then they are thirsty. The list is endless. It can be exhausting for both the child and parents.

From the Horse's Mouth

The issue of sleeping alone in their bed can be a difficult one for so many children, particularly those who struggle with anxiety. Even for adults, everything can look more frightening when you wake in the middle of the night. I could always understand why a child, anxious or not, might need the reassurance of a parent's touch when the world seems a scary place. I remember a friend telling me that her little girl once asked why her mum and dad were allowed to share a bed when she, who got scared more easily, had to sleep alone. My friend struggled to answer the question, and I must admit, it stopped me in my tracks, too.

We know routines and rituals help our children to feel safe and secure. They bring comfort and security at times of transition when life seems difficult. They remind our children that their home life is a predictable and safe environment. Starting a bedtime routine can help support children who struggle with anxiety to settle down to sleep. Make sure that no matter who puts the child to bed, the same routine is followed each night. Your child will get used to winding down each evening as soon as the routine starts. Starting with a warm bath or a warm drink before you ever get to the bedroom can be a good way to start. You can prepare the bedroom for sleep as they get into their nightclothes after their bath. Dim the light, perhaps use a night light, maybe have soothing music playing, or light a scented candle.

☝ Give it a Try!

Here is an example of a bedtime routine to give you some ideas. But sitting with your child and agreeing a bedtime routine to follow can help with security:

- Take a warm bath, brush your teeth, and get dressed for bed.
- Read a story for about ten minutes to help you settle.
- Think of three things or people that you are grateful for that day.
- Look around your room and focus on three things that make you happy.
- Close your eyes and do your 'belly breathing' until you feel drowsy.

Remember, your child can also use their favourite self-regulation tools to help them relax and go to sleep, whether it is breathing, a body scan, or even a comfort toy. In Guatemala, there is a tradition of teaching children to tell their worries to *Worry Dolls*. These are small, colourful, hand-made dolls clothed in traditional Mayan costumes that the child can say their concerns to. The story of the worry doll comes from a Mayan legend about a princess who received a special gift from the sun god that allowed her to solve all human problems. The child tells their worries to the dolls, and the dolls will worry for the child while they sleep peacefully. The legend is that by morning, the dolls will have given you what you need to solve or face that worry. Worry dolls can be very effective for children who are prevented from going to sleep by worrying about everything in their lives.

If you have a child who struggles to let you leave the bedroom, you can address this by taking baby steps away from them. This is very similar to the laddering process we covered earlier. After their bedtime routine, start by sitting on the bed as they are going to sleep, and explain to them that you will wait until they go to sleep.

You won't sneak off and leave them, but it is time for sleep, so you cannot chat with them. Do this for a few nights, then move to sit on a chair beside the bed for a few nights. Again, reassure them you will wait until they go to sleep. In another few nights, sit further away in the bedroom, and a few nights later, sit at the bedroom door. After that, sit outside the door. You are slowly moving further and further away from them. Work out individual steps based on your child. The process takes time and patience. However, this method of moving away from them in incremental steps helps them develop a sense of security as they go to sleep.

One issue to mention when considering sleep for our teens is social media, as we know that social media use impacts their sleep time. The light emitted by phone screens suppresses the sleep hormone melatonin. That means it can be difficult to fall asleep after a period of interacting on their phones. Our teens who struggle with anxiety need to become very protective about their sleep routines and try to step away from social media at least an hour before bedtime.

👍 Give it a Try!

Here are some things to try when encouraging your child or teen to develop better sleep habits:

- Avoid eating or drinking anything with high sugar content in the evening.
- Develop a set sleep routine every evening (for example, little ones can include a bath, story, breathing exercises, and a body scan. Older children can shower, read, or listen to music, followed by breathing exercises).
- Stick to similar go-to-bed and wake-up times throughout the week (so no long weekend lie-ins for teens).

- For older children, stick to a 'no mobile phones in the bedroom' rule. Encourage older teens to come off their phones an hour before sleep and keep their phones 'silent' at nighttime so they don't hear notifications. Even better, have a 'charging station' in your kitchen where all the family leave their mobile phones overnight.

The Science of Movement and Happiness

There is a wealth of evidence to support the assertion that engaging in physical activity impacts our mental health. We know that the benefits of physical exercise have a neurochemical basis. Exercise decreases stress hormones like cortisol and adrenaline. Physical activity will also decrease cortisol levels at night, which will benefit children who struggle with sleep. Furthermore, it stimulates the production of endorphins, the body's feel-good chemicals. These are the body's natural mood elevators. Even as adults, most of us are familiar with the feelings of optimism and positivity we experience after a workout or even a walk.

Encouraging your child to engage in some form of exercise can help release tensions and endorphins and will help their overall wellbeing. Often, when a child feels anxious, they are more inclined to retreat into themselves rather than get up and get active. But remember, exercise should be fun. It does not have to be something we force them to take part in. Very often, it is when they are least in the mood that they really need the benefits of movement. The more fun the activity is, the more likely the child is to engage in it.

It is recommended that children six years and older engage in an hour of moderate physical activity every day. This can be engaging in any form of sports activity or active play that gets their heart rate up. In addition to this, they should be encouraged to engage in more vigorous pursuits, like formal sports activities, a few times a week. They should also engage in additional light physical activity, such as walking to and from school.

The science of movement and happiness tells us that anything our children enjoy that gets their bodies moving is good for their wellbeing. Whether it is jumping on the trampoline, dancing to their favourite songs, rollerblading, or taking a yoga class, just getting them moving will usually improve their mood. There are clearly physical benefits, too, in terms of building strength and muscle tone, joint and bone development, and supporting coordination skills. But the social and emotional skills are also many, from fostering teamwork and friendships in organised sports to boosting self-esteem and resilience and developing problem-solving and conflict resolution skills in free play activities.

We know that participation in physical exercise drops as children approach their teenage years, especially for girls. However, studies have also shown that lifestyles developed in childhood are more likely to continue through the lifespan. If we can build sports and physical activities into family life when our children are younger, they are more likely to continue to have physical activity as part of their lifestyle. One of the best ways to encourage younger children to exercise is to make it a family affair. Find activities that you enjoy taking part in as a family. If getting physical exercise is part of your family routine, it becomes an accepted part of family life. It is also beneficial to let your children see you engage in activities yourself, whether it is taking an exercise class or even taking a walk with friends.

When considering physical activity, don't underestimate the impact of getting out in nature. We know that interactions with nature can positively affect wellbeing. However, in our modern world, many of us are disconnected from nature. A growing body of evidence supports the idea that exposure to natural environments, such as beaches, parks, or woodlands, is associated with greater positive wellbeing. Various research projects have found many benefits, such as improved cardiovascular health, lower levels of obesity and diabetes, and improved mental health in both adults and children. More time spent in nature is also associated with better self-reported health and wellbeing in adults. We know that there are consequences to our children's detachment from the world of nature. It results in both a reduction in physical and emotional wellbeing but also a lowering of their sense of belonging and personal identity within the world.

Not only spending time in nature but caring for it, for example, growing flowers and vegetables and taking care of animals, helps children to see their role in relation to the world around them. You don't need access to a large garden. Children can grow flowers, herbs, or some vegetables by planting a small patch in the garden or in containers on a balcony. Planting seeds, feeding, watering them, and watching them grow gives children a sense of responsibility and purpose. Because gardening is such a slow process, it helps children to understand that not everything brings instant gratification, but good things come to those who wait. Seeing their seeds grow and enjoying the herbs or flowers they have planted gives them a sense of their capability.

Nature can generate a multitude of positive emotions. Importantly, one of those is a sense of calm. Something most of our children who struggle with anxiety really could benefit from. Not all of us are lucky enough to have easy access to nature. If this is the case for your family, try to focus on everyday aspects of nature closer to home.

Surprisingly, even watching nature documentaries is good for our mental health. For anyone who has limited access to nature, keep this in mind. Even making a habit of watching documentaries like *The Blue Planet* with our children is building an association with the world around them.

Two research studies by the Max Planck Institute for Human Development published in 2022 suggest that listening to birdsong is good for our mental wellbeing. In the first study[28], researchers found a significant positive association between seeing or hearing birds, with continued improved mental wellbeing reported up to four hours later. Interestingly, these 'bird benefits' were felt by healthy participants and those diagnosed with depression, reinforcing the idea that nature has healing properties. The second study found that listening to short audio clips of birdsong reduced feelings of anxiety, depression, and paranoia[29]. They noted that listening to birdsong through headphones was able to hit the same pathways that alleviate negative emotions. This research makes clear that even if we don't have access to nature all the time, listening to the noises of nature, such as birdsong, can have a positive impact on our mood.

Conclusion

In today's society, we so often expect instantaneous results. But, if we want to see change in our children's lives, we need to take a series of small steps and maintain them consistently over time to improve their response to anxiety.

In his book *The Compound Effect*, Darren Hardy[30] speaks about how taking small actions, maintained in a consistent way, can lead to success. The small daily decisions we make have a direct impact on the direction our lives take. He outlines two examples in the book to explain this. The first is an example from finance, where he explains that compound interest can lead to large returns. If you were offered a choice between taking $3 million in cash now or a single penny that doubles in value every day for 31 days, which would you take? He explains that the penny ends up being worth over $10 million. The second is the story of three friends, one of whom starts making small, seemingly inconsequential changes to his lifestyle. He reads ten pages of a good book each day, listens to something inspirational on his way to work, and cuts 125 calories from his daily diet. The other two friends make very small but poor choices. Little change is seen between the three friends five months later, or indeed ten months later. But after two years, while the other two friends have declined in various ways, the friend who made these small but positive changes has seen dramatic effects in his physical and mental health.

Basically, small steps lead to major progress. Think of this as you encourage your child to start making small but positive choices, which will, over time, have a big impact on their anxiety.

CHAPTER 6

Looking At Ourselves

'I'm afraid,' said Rabbit.
'What are you afraid of?' asked Bear.
'I don't know,' Rabbit replied. 'I'm just scared.'
'So, I will sit next to you until you stop being afraid,' said Bear.
'We will face it together.'

Tara Shannon[31]

As parents, we want the best for our children, but when they are struggling, we often look inwards. Instead of blaming ourselves for our children's anxiety, let's remember the complexity of our children's development. In psychology, we used to talk about the nature-nurture debate. However, more recently, when talking about anxiety, as with so many other issues, we speak about it being interactionist. What does this mean? It is an interaction between nature and nurture. There may be a genetic predisposition to anxiety for some children, but we cannot discount our environment. Most generational anxiety is a combination of an innate tendency and the impact of learned behaviour. We are not in control of the paths our children will take, but we can be an influence.

For most of us, their anxiety has changed how we interact with our children. Often, without really realising it, we adapt and modify our behaviours to try to reduce our child's anxiety. To help them deal with anxiety, we have fallen into preventative strategies which can, at times, accommodate their anxiety. We may have given in to pleas for support during anxiety-provoking situations, and we may have become more protective than we would wish in our goal of defeating anxious thoughts. I know I have been guilty of both of the above. It can help to consider our role as partners to our child so that we can better overcome anxiety.

Common Parenting Traps

Let's start by looking at some common traps we often fall into. Notice I am using the word 'we' here, so please, if you can relate to these things, don't feel you are alone. These are our natural responses to our children's anxiety.

• It'll be Grand

The first mistake we often make is to reassure the child that there is no need to be anxious. Have you ever heard yourself saying, 'Don't be silly. It'll be grand,' or 'There is absolutely nothing to worry about.'

This doesn't work. We know there is nothing to worry about, so we assure them there is nothing to worry about. Your anxious child would love to believe you, but their brain is in overdrive. You are appealing to that higher-level thinking area of the brain, but remember, the amygdala is in control. We have all heard the saying, no one has ever calmed down by being told to calm down. Well, it's true.

Instead of trying to 'fix' our child's anxiety, our first response should be to stop. Stop what we are doing, stop talking, stop trying to make it all better. We know that our children cannot think logically when caught up in the fight or flight response, yet we often try to reason with them instead of responding in a supportive manner. Instead of trying to connect with their thinking brain, showing empathy can connect with their emotional brain. Even if we cannot understand the reason for their anxiety, we are connecting with the feeling they are experiencing and letting them know we understand that this is hard for them. Then, a few words, asking if there is anything you can do to help or if they would like you to take some deep breaths with them, may provide comfort.

What we really want our children to understand is that they are so much more than their anxiety. If they can stop and pause and allow those tricky emotions to run over them, the anxiety will pass. Anxiety is not who they are, although, at times, it may feel as if the anxiety has knocked them off their feet. But if they let it flow through them, they will stand again. This is such an important message for our children who are struggling and for those of us caught up in the storm with them.

• Constant Reassurance

There can be a tendency with children who struggle with anxiety to constantly seek reassurance from their parents. They may ask about the same situation again and again, needing assurance that everything is OK. As parents, we want to tell our children that their world is safe, and indeed, such comfort can provide temporary relief. However, the need for constant reassurance is not a helpful way of dealing with anxiety, as it can result in a child who is dependent on others. We would prefer them to learn to trust themselves.

To be honest, a child needing constant reassurance can also be exhausting for parents. If this rings any bells when thinking of your own child, instead of providing reassurance, focus on the anxiety. Saying something like, 'As you are asking me these questions, I wonder if this is your anxiety speaking? Could we do something to make you feel less worried about this?' Then maybe do some slow breathing or another relaxation exercise. Moving from constant reassurance to letting the child know that they can take an active stance against these thoughts reminds them that they can manage their anxiety in a healthier way.

☝ Give it a Try!

Instead of constant reassurance, we can normalise their anxiety, validate their feelings, and show faith in them. What does that look like in real life? **Normalise** by saying something like, 'It is only natural that you feel nervous about going back to school after a long break. I would feel exactly the same way.' Then, **Validate** their feelings. 'I know it can be hard to settle back into a routine when you have had a break. It can feel a little scary for a while as you get back on track.' Then, show **Faith** in their competence by saying something like, 'I am right here to support you. I remember you felt this way after the break last year, but I also remember how well you settled in once you started.'

• Reinforcing Fears

We also sometimes unintentionally reinforce our children's fears. Although we don't want to belittle a child's anxiety, we don't want to amplify it. For example, your child is frightened of dogs, and you show anxiety yourself if you see a dog approaching and rush your child in the opposite direction. In this way, we are giving our child more reason to believe there is something to be anxious about.

Linked to this is trying to over-prepare our children. Sometimes, we talk about what's ahead far too early. Try instead to keep anticipatory periods short. It is not that we don't want to acknowledge their fears, but the message we want to give is one of support. Instead of amplifying their anxiety, we want to acknowledge it and let them know we will help them get through this.

We sometimes equate worry with love but remember, our worry does not protect our child. Worry is passive and will not solve any of our children's anxieties. It can result in us becoming overprotective and controlling. It can also result in us constantly talking about the issues at hand, which can amplify anxiety. Keep this in mind when you are worried about your child.

If you are caught in a cycle of worry, take a break instead and join your child for a period of play. It is difficult to worry when you are deeply engaged in play with your child. Play instead reinforces our connection with our child.

Remember, what our children need from us when anxiety is threatening to overwhelm them is our comfort. We need to be the port in the storm. The reminder that they have what they need right inside them, even though they might not be able to see it right now.

• Shouting

When our children seem to be regressing or going back into anxious patterns, we can sometimes allow our frustration to boil over and end up shouting at them. When I talk to parents about not shouting at their children, I worry that I am adding to the stress of already stressed parents. But it is important to mention the link between shouting and shame.

Although our goal should be to try not to shout at our children, there are different types of shouting. If you would call yourself a 'shouty mum' as a mother recently told me she calls herself, ask yourself why you are shouting. There is a difference between yelling up the stairs at your child to hurry up as you are rushing out the door and shouting at your child, 'Do you not understand anything? How often do I have to tell you what to do?' The first might not be helpful, but the second is belittling and shaming the child. This is the type of shouting that the research tells us is damaging to our children.

However, for most of us, if we lose our patience with our child, we need to remind ourselves that we are only human. Empathise with yourself. Even good parents shout sometimes. Then, empathise with the child in front of you and repair. This will help to reconnect after a disconnect. When you are calm, go back and tell them that you are so sorry that you shouted and that you are working hard at staying calm, even when you feel frustrated. Let them know you spoke out of anger and would like to make things better. Let them know you are working on doing better in future.

Apologising to our children is not a sign of weakness. It is a sign of strength. It is modelling the behaviour we would expect of them if they have done something they regret and are sorry for. Children who are apologised to become children who apologise to others. We are letting our children know that we all mess up sometimes, but when we do, we will apologise and work harder to do better in future.

Top Tip!

We often talk about trying to *Practise the Pause* when you feel frustration rising within your body. Just taking a moment to pause and breathe can help us to reset. If you are feeling stress levels rising, a good tip to help you pause is to either wash your hands with cold water or splash cold water on your face before responding. It gives you a second to pause and de-escalate before you react to your child. Water can also help to calm some children when they are feeling anxious. Water play or playing in the bath can help soothe stress levels.

- **Avoidance**

Finally, the most important thing to avoid is avoidance itself. Your child will usually want to avoid the situation causing anxiety. The flight part of the fight or flight response urges you to escape the threatening situation. Avoidance is a perfectly natural response to the physical manifestation of anxiety. Why wouldn't our children want to escape from these awful feelings? It makes perfect sense to get away. But this is a dangerous approach because it seems to work. Helping children avoid the things they are afraid of will make them feel better in the short term, but it reinforces the anxiety in the long run. The child will never learn that he can cope with this anxiety. As parents, we instinctually protect our children from anxiety, so we often allow them to side-step the situations which make them anxious. But by doing this, we are inadvertently telling the child that this situation is one they should be fearful of.

Mark Smyth, Senior Clinical Psychologist with Child and Adolescent Mental Health Services (CAMHS), uses the children's story 'We're Going on A Bear Hunt' by Michael Rosen as an example when he speaks about anxiety. In the story, a family decide to go out one morning to hunt for a bear. In their search, they come across various obstacles. They must face long, wavy grass, a deep, cold river, thick, oozy mud, a big dark forest, and a snowstorm. Facing each obstacle, the children feel anxious and wonder how they are going to cope. They chant a rhyme, reminding themselves that they are not scared. While crossing each obstacle, they chant that they *can't go over it*, they *can't go under it*, and they realise that the only way to overcome each fear is to *go through it*. Finally, the children go through all the obstacles and find a bear, who is indeed frightening and chases them home. This time, on returning through all the obstacles, they move quickly through them to get home. This time, they are more prepared to face each obstacle as they have already experienced it once. Mark reminds parents what an important message this is for our children.

The best way to help children overcome anxiety isn't to remove all the stressors that trigger it. Instead, it is to support them to face the situations that make them afraid. This will help them to function as well as they can, even when they're anxious, and will result in a long-term decrease in anxiety.

From the Horse's Mouth

I know that I have been guilty of supporting my child, who struggles with anxiety and avoidance. A few questions I have found helpful in challenging my own beliefs about this type of 'support' are:

- Do I believe that facing this fear will cause harm to my child?
- Do I believe that she is able to cope with facing this fear?
- Am I supporting her to avoid this situation because it is impacting my own fears for her?

Sometimes, our distress at seeing our child face a situation causes us to accommodate their fears. Asking these questions can help us consider whether this distress is holding us back from supporting them to move forward.

Avoidance teaches the amygdala that staying away from anxiety works. However, the amygdala only learns from experience. It needs to practise repetition to take on board new habits. It is very probable that your child has learned to avoid what makes them anxious, so we need to very slowly teach the amygdala that this is not the way to go. If your child has been avoiding anxiety for some time, the process can be challenging. The amygdala will fight this, so anxiety can seem to get worse before it gets better. But rather than allowing avoidance because we worry about what might happen and the impact of our decisions, let's encourage our children to take small chances and baby steps - just as we discussed earlier with the *Fear Ladder* and the *Imagined Edge*.

In his book *Actualisations*[32], Stewart Emery speaks about our fears when we consider changing direction in our lives. He tells a story about a flight he took to Honolulu when he was on the flight deck and was speaking to the pilot about the flight instruments. The pilot advised him that one of these was called the Inertial Guidance System. The purpose of this system is to get the plane to the runway in Hawaii in the allocated time slot. On departure, the flight path is input into the computer, and each time the plane strays off course, this system corrects it. The pilot explained to Emery that despite being slightly off course for 90% of the journey, the plane would arrive safely in Hawaii due to this system. As Emery explains, the original flight path is set accurately. If the flight veers off the path, the system corrects it. If it veers off again, it is corrected again, and this pattern continues until near landing. He relates this example to our plans in life. Often, we have a goal in life but spend so much time worrying that we might veer off course. Instead, he recommends we accept that we may veer off course many times. Don't worry about making wrong decisions. Instead, learn to correct when necessary.

What a message for us as parents, and an important message to share with our children who struggle with anxiety. Let's avoid avoidance and, instead, encourage our children to take small steps outside their comfort zone. If they are worried about the impact of this, remind them not to worry about veering off course. They can always auto correct.

☝ Give it a Try!

Stop for a moment and consider if your child pushes you to change your behaviour to allow them to avoid anxiety-provoking situations:

- Have they asked you to contact a teacher or sports coach on their behalf because they didn't want to ask a question themselves?
- Have they asked you to do a household task for them because they want to avoid anxious feelings?

- Have they asked you to lie about illness so they can avoid going to an event?
- Have they asked you to contact another parent to speak about their child so they can avoid dealing with a minor friendship issue?
- Have they asked you to do something else developmentally appropriate for their age group because it makes them feel anxious to do it?

Take the time to consider how your child asks you to support them in avoiding situations that create anxiety and if the situation that you were supporting them to avoid was, in fact, dangerous or intolerable. Did this strategy work, but only in the short term?

Avoidance, even if it temporarily removes anxiety, reduces your child's ability to cope long-term. I am not saying that we take an old-fashioned approach of telling our children to 'man up' (a term I hate) and face their fears head-on. No, instead of avoidance, I am suggesting that we encourage baby steps towards bravery.

Pushing Beyond the Comfort Zone

I was once told that the comfort zone is a beautiful place, but nothing ever grows there. It rang very true for me, particularly when considering our children who struggle with anxiety. Sitting in our comfort zone is a very anxiety-neutral position. We feel calm and safe. Although routine and stability are important for our children, some of them need encouragement to come out of their comfort zone, particularly those who struggle with anxiety. When their decisions are based on fear, they miss out on many life experiences. They need to find the balance between comfort and risk, and by encouraging them to step out into the world, we help them to persevere with life's challenges. Taking small steps and giving them the support they need to try new things can help them build confidence and resilience.

 ## Learning From Psychology

Psychologist Lev Vygotsky coined the term *Zone of Proximal Development* (ZPD) when considering how parents and carers can support children's learning and development. The ZPD is important to consider when we want to push children outside their comfort zone. It is the level just beyond a child's current capacity, a zone of growth sitting just outside the comfort zone. Vygotsky argued that this zone is a level of achievement or mastery that a child can accomplish with the support of a more knowledgeable other. The level of adult guidance is adjusted according to the level of the child's performance. This guidance enables the child to achieve a skill they would not have been able to attain alone. In essence, with a little guidance from us, maximum growth can happen. Vygotsky stressed the importance of gently pushing children within this zone but not into a zone where they are so far beyond their reach that they cannot achieve. In this zone, he argued that children become a head taller than themselves.

I speak about pushing your child outside the comfort zone as if it is an easy thing to do. But often, instead, our protective instincts kick in, and we feel awful about encouraging our children towards what makes them anxious. It feels completely counterintuitive. Sometimes, we need to find our inner bravery so that they can find theirs. Remember, every step is a step towards a less anxious life.

☝ Give it a Try!

For a child who avoids going outside their comfort zone, a small activity that can help them is to try something new every day for a month. Get them to pick one thing to do outside their comfort zone every day. Depending on the age of the child, this could be something like cooking a meal by themselves, trying a new sport, learning a new card game, walking to a friend's house, going into a shop by themselves, taking a mindfulness class, walking the dog by themselves, or camping out in the back garden. Anything at all that is a little beyond what they are used to. They can keep a little adventure diary of everything new they try and how they get on.

Something your child might not understand or might not believe, but which is true, is that pushing through their anxiety is less frightening than living with that constant anxiety and the feelings of helplessness that it brings. The most difficult step is the first one. If they are supported to take that first step, the rest get easier over time. Each time we move outside our comfort zone, our confidence increases, and we become more powerful.

A growing body of research has begun to examine the area of 'challenging parenting behaviour' and whether it is a buffer against anxiety in children. Challenging parenting behaviour includes encouraging children to take risks, encouraging them to explore unfamiliar situations with confidence, encouraging children to be assertive, and to engage in rough and tumble play. We know that children of parents who help them push boundaries are less likely to struggle with anxiety disorders, reminding us to encourage our children to push their limits.

This is something I know that I, and many other parents, battle with. Often, the first thing our child will ask us to do is to help them overcome anxiety by removing stressors. Instead, we need to support our children to function as well as they can, even when anxious. We can challenge ourselves to display confidence in our children, particularly when they or we are feeling anxious about a situation.

We know that children can learn to 'get used to' anxiety, following on from our understanding of the habituation curve. Habituation basically means the process of becoming accustomed to a situation. If you imagine jumping into a swimming pool for the first time, the water temperature usually feels cold. But as we stay in the water, we feel as if the water has warmed up. In fact, the temperature hasn't become warmer. We have just become used to it or habituated to it. The same happens with anxiety. When we are exposed to an anxiety-provoking situation, our anxiety steadily increases. But if we can sit with that anxiety, it reduces over time. Without us doing anything, the anxiety decreases. The more we expose ourselves to the anxiety-provoking situation, the less anxiety it provokes. This is called anxiety habituation.

If we don't gently push our children out of their comfort zones, avoidance becomes their go-to response to anxiety. There is a very real danger that the child will shrink away from the world and retreat into the safety of their home or room. Clearly, that is not what we want for our children. We cannot tell them that life is always safe, but we can remind them that when they are trying to find the courage that we know they have within them, we will be there with them, supporting them.

From the Horse's Mouth

When we are encouraging our children to push beyond their comfort zones, it can help if we can model brave behaviour ourselves. As I have mentioned, I have a fear of heights and try to avoid heights when possible. However (hypocritically, you may say!) I try to encourage my child, who struggles with anxiety, to face her fears. We were at a theme park that had a tree top skywalk, and she managed to completely turn the tables on me. She encouraged me to find my inner brave and take on the skywalk with her. Terrified as I was, I had to try, or she would never listen to me encouraging her to be brave again. I would never have managed it without her. She did the course backwards, facing me, encouraging me to take every step, much to the entertainment of everyone watching below. But what a feeling of exhilaration having completed the course. I am not saying I would rush back to do it again, but it made me realise that I can take on more than I believed. It also showed my daughter that although I urge her to try to move beyond her comfort zone, I expect the same of myself. Finally, it also made her realise that sometimes I need her to support me when something makes me anxious, too.

Anxiety and bravery are inextricably linked, but often, the anxious child forgets that. Our children who struggle with anxiety are brave every day. Sometimes, getting out of bed in the morning to face the world takes bravery. We can remind them of the strength they have internally while also equipping them with tools to help them be brave when they don't feel it. Remember, their connection with us can give them the strength they need to face their fears. Each time your child takes another challenging step, they will eventually learn to cope with that situation, and you raise the bar ever so slightly again.

Fitness professionals speak about the concept of progressive overload when their clients are working towards building strength in the gym. The idea of this strength-building principle is that to build muscle you need to progressively add repetitions to your workout and increase weights to make incremental gains. As your body adapts and you get stronger with each increase, you repeat the cycle again. The idea is that when you are in your comfort zone during a workout, you will plateau as your body is no longer being challenged. To become stronger, your muscles must continue to work harder and harder over time. This principle can be applied to working through anxiety.

Someone engaging in strength training, as described above, should also have a recovery strategy after each workout, whether it is a stretching session, a massage, or indeed, to refuel and rehydrate. Similarly, our children should have a way to replenish their reserves after pushing themselves outside their comfort zone. It could be spending time with their dog, taking a bath, or snuggling with us on the sofa. This will help them to decompress after taking on a challenge. We want them to gently stretch themselves beyond their familiar limits to enable them to develop resilience.

The Second Chicken

Psychologist Lawrence Cohen tells the story of how chickens use tonic immobilisation (basically freezing and playing dead) when threatened by predators[33]. If a chicken fears a threat, it will play dead for about a minute. However, Cohen found that if that chicken sees a second chicken who also fears a danger, the two chickens will play dead for up to five minutes. It is as if the first chicken thinks to himself, 'Well, if that chicken thinks something is wrong, I must be missing something, so I better play dead for longer.' However, if the second chicken is walking around happily, the first chicken pops back up very quickly. This time, it seems to think, 'Well, if that guy thinks everything is OK, it must be OK.' In essence, the message is that a scared chicken looks at the second chicken to see if the world is safe. Cohen found that chickens stayed immobilised for the longest when they looked in a mirror and thought their frozen reflection was another scared chicken.

He relates this to children who struggle with anxiety and the responses of their parents. I suppose the question we ask ourselves as parents is, 'How can we make sure we are not that scared second chicken?' Even if we reassure our child that nothing is wrong, as we noted earlier, logic will not work when a child is in a state of heightened anxiety. Instead, Cohen suggests we ask our children, 'Would you look in my eyes and see whether or not I'm scared?' He suggests this works much better than simple reassurance that everything is fine, as it brings them into the present and helps them feel your projection of calm confidence.

When our children are anxious, they will look to us for reassurance. If they see us looking concerned, it seems to confirm to them that the world is indeed not a safe place. They are right to be scared.

From the Horse's Mouth

I remember when I initially read about the second chicken, thinking to myself, 'Well, that can't be me. I'm not that anxious a parent. I don't think I parent my children in a very anxious way.' But then I realised I don't parent my three children in the same way. I have come to understand that I parent my child who struggles with anxiety in a more anxious way than the other two. And I don't think I am alone. I believe that when our child starts to struggle with anxiety, it awakens instincts within us that leave us in a state of high alert. But when the world seems a scary place, the most important thing our children need from us is calm. We need to be aware of that inner voice that tells us to jump in and fix every worry—that parental instinct to rescue our children from all anxiety. By saving them, with that fearful look in our eyes, we are telling them that they are not capable of saving themselves. We may not be able to control the world, but we can control our responses. That is where our power lies.

It is so easy to fall into the trap of accommodating anxious feelings. We change family routines or behaviours due to one child in the family feeling anxious. We become so involved in our child's anxiety that we negatively reinforce it. Without realising it, we are telling our children that they are right to feel anxious. Their internal alarm is right. For example, if my child is anxious about the first day of school, and she sees me getting tearful about leaving her in the classroom, I am telling her that she is right to think this place holds danger. She is right to feel fear and apprehension, as her mother is feeling it, too. I am reinforcing a danger that does not, in reality, exist.

👍 Give it a Try!

If you are finding yourself lying awake at night in a cycle of worry about your child, remember this is not working to solve the problem. If you are lying awake with your brain spinning, going over and over your worries, try putting a notepad beside your bed and writing down any ideas that might solve the problem. Writing the problem down tends to lift the worry off your shoulders. It can help you to feel less overwhelmed and more in control of the situation as you clear your mind and put some order to your thoughts.

Eli Lebowitz and colleagues at Yale School of Medicine have considered this issue in depth[34]. They have developed a programme called SPACE (Supportive Parenting for Anxious Childhood Emotions), which is a treatment aimed at parents of children with anxiety. The programme is based on the tenet that reducing parent's accommodation of childhood anxiety will help children learn to cope better themselves. Our constant accommodations, they argue, lead to our children becoming over-reliant on parents to solve all their problems. The programme teaches parents how to step back from their child, supporting them to manage their anxiety themselves. The idea is that exposing our children to frustration while also showing confidence in their ability to cope with our gentle support will better support them to function in an anxious world.

Just one proviso here. Lebowitz acknowledges that the SPACE programme is not a 'cure-all' for every child. He notes children with severe anxiety, those who are unable to attend school, for example, need a different level of intervention and greater support. However, he believes that for children with milder anxiety, for example, those who are anxious about attending school but who can still attend every day, removing accommodations and replacing them with supportive messages can be very effective.

 **Top Tip!**

If you find yourself feeling anxious about your child's anxiety, stop for a moment and take a few deep breaths. Then ask yourself, what is the worst that might happen, and how likely is it that this will, in fact, happen? Take a moment to consider if this is a real or imagined fear.

Remember, it takes time to support a child who is struggling with anxiety. You are not only supporting them with the tools to change their response to anxious feelings, but you are also working towards changing your own responses, too.

Reflective Listening

Instead of jumping in to try to fix the world for our children, we can instead take on the role of listener. Our children often want us to listen and acknowledge their feelings rather than try to solve every problem. Reflective listening is one way we can ensure our children feel heard, ensuring that we are giving them the time and attention that they deserve. This involves not only listening but repeating back to the child our interpretation of what they have said. This helps us to fully understand the points they are making but also communicate this back to them. It shows the child that we have fully listened to what they are saying without judgement.

Here are the steps involved in *Reflective Listening*:

- Start by asking the child how they are feeling, then take the time to fully listen to their responses. Focus on understanding the message rather than making any judgements.
- Try to analyse what the child is telling you objectively. Repeat back to them your understanding of what they have said in a gentle voice. Try to explain more than the facts presented but also your understanding of the emotions they are expressing.
- Use encouraging phrases to further develop the discussion, for example, 'Can you tell me a little more about that?' or 'I am wondering, are you saying...?'
- Allow the child to confirm back that you have fully understood their viewpoint.

When you are engaged in reflective listening you should not only pay attention to the language your child uses but also to their body language. Sometimes, a child will tell you they are not bothered about a situation, while their body language might tell you otherwise. When their words and body language tell you two different things, always believe the body language.

A Word on Perfection

Some of our children who struggle with anxiety have set very unrealistic goals for themselves and are constantly evaluating themselves in critical ways. They are perfectionists who judge themselves very harshly. If they do not meet their very high expectations for success, this is deemed as failure – in their world, mistakes are unacceptable. If you have noticed that your child sets unrealistic standards for themselves, becomes upset at minor errors, can't tolerate criticism well, or checks work excessively, they may well be struggling with perfectionism. Evaluating themselves in highly critical ways can easily lead to anxiety.

A study of college students in the US, the UK, and Canada found that rates of socially prescribed perfectionism have increased over the past few decades, rising by a third from the nineties to the present day[35]. This type of perfectionism is characterised by the fear of failing to meet the expectations of others. The study found that recent generations of young people perceive that others are more demanding of them, that they are also more demanding of others, and more demanding of themselves than previous generations. The authors attribute some of this to competitive individualism across the Western world, resulting in our young people striving to achieve personal perfection.

This research reminds us that so many of our teens today feel under pressure to meet the high expectations that society puts them under. They feel they should be able to achieve well academically, live up to very demanding social expectations, and present a perfect body image online. They are being judged by exam results, how they look, their popularity on social media, and their families' finances. The list is never-ending. Even if we believe that we, as parents, are not putting them under this pressure, society places pressure on them to achieve. They are constantly being given the message that they are not enough just as they are. They need to strive harder, do better, and achieve more. Their academic achievement, social standing, and popularity are measures of their personal worth.

Rising competitiveness in society today can lead to a crisis in confidence for many children. When will they ever live up to the expectations that are placed on them? These feelings of judgement can lead them to be overcritical of themselves, fearing imperfection. To support a child who thinks this way, it is important to challenge these perfectionist tendencies.

We can counteract this by experimenting with 'non-perfectionist' behaviour with our children. Encourage them to use an exposure and response type activity to cope with the anxiety that non-perfection brings. This involves them deliberately doing something less than perfectly. For example, if they keep erasing their schoolwork until they feel it is perfect, try to get them to submit it on the first draft. If they do not try out for the school team because they feel they will not be the best player, encourage them to give it a try. If they insist on checking every maths question on their calculator to make sure their answers are correct, encourage them to trust their ability. If they ask you to brush, brush, and brush their hair every morning until they feel it is perfect, encourage them to put it in a ponytail after the first brush. Any opportunity you can find to get them to do something 'less well' will help them see that they can cope with minor errors and that they are not the end of the world.

When considering perfectionism, it is also important to consider the motivation for our children and teens, most importantly, whether they are working to achieve intrinsic or extrinsic aspirations. Intrinsic motivation comes from within. This motivation relates to areas such as personal satisfaction, personal development, and an internal desire to complete a goal. Extrinsic motivation relates to external validation. You are doing something to gain external rewards, goals such as money, fame, or power. It is the difference between playing a sport because you love the game and only participating when you feel your team will win a match. It is the difference between learning a language because you want to communicate on holiday and learning a language to pass an exam. It is the difference between spending time with a friend because you enjoy their company and spending time with people you do not connect with but have greater social standing.

Prof Jean Twenge from the University of San Diego has examined intrinsic and extrinsic motivation in students and found that this generation is moving from more *intrinsic* goals (such as personal growth or core values) to *extrinsic* goals (such as public image or financial gain)[36]. If my personal satisfaction comes from the views or rewards of others, it can make my life more difficult. Twenge argues these changes are due to a preoccupation with material gain and social image. This generation has been repeatedly bombarded with images online that focus on looking good, being popular, and having material possessions. From a young age, the message has been ingrained in them that success depends on popularity, looks, and wealth. They are the generation who value image over substance and view success as linked to Instagram followers. The image you portray is more important than the person you are.

For parents, dealing with perfectionism also involves looking at ourselves. Childhood should be about learning through play, a time of exploration, discovering the world on their own terms, and a time of joyfulness. If we create an atmosphere in our homes where perfection is expected, childhood becomes a more anxious time. Our children spend their days feeling that they should be living up to our expectations of them and fearful of not living up to those hopes.

Remember, we do not have to be a perfect parent. We know that no such thing exists. However, the level of judgement of our parenting skills today is very high. We are particularly aware of this judgement when our children are struggling. Just as societal pressure is on us to perform to a very idealised standard in our parenting, the pressure is on us to produce children who are flawless, too. When our children struggle in some way, we often feel that this reflects on us as parents - as though we aren't doing our job properly. This can lead us to be very controlling in our parenting. We need to jump in and help our children with every struggle. That is the only way we are sure it will be handled perfectly. We can be highly critical of ourselves and of our children. Instead of working towards success, we constantly focus on avoiding failure. If any of this resonates with you, it is important to have the courage to allow yourself to be imperfect. Sometimes, we need to consider our critical inner voices. Practise some self-compassion and allow yourself to be perfectly imperfect.

Conclusion

Rather than allow anxiety to become the most important member of our household, controlling both our lives and the lives of our children, we need to turn that situation on its head. We need to encourage our child to face some of their fears to give them the opportunities they need for positive coping. We can actively support our children to reduce the behaviours that protect them from experiencing anxiety. Instead, we can normalise anxiety, reduce accommodations, and encourage them to take baby steps towards a less anxious life. An important way we can do this is to encourage our children to tolerate uncertainty and take responsible risks, resulting in a more resilient child.

CHAPTER 7

Resilience and Risk

Parents are one of the most important influences on children's resilience.
Instead of a focus on keeping our children as safe as possible, it may help if we reframe this as keeping them as safe as necessary. We cannot promise that they will never face challenging situations. But we can let them see our faith in their ability to cope.

Dr Mary O'Kane

As much as we would like to smooth every path for our children, it is in their best interests to become independent and take responsibility for their own lives.

Resilience has been getting a bit of a bad rap lately, with some commentators claiming that it is used as an excuse to place responsibility on the child to deal with difficult circumstances, even if they are trauma-inducing. This is most definitely not what resilience should be about.

Others refer to resilience as the ability to 'bounce back' from adversity. Again, I take issue with this analogy. For me, there is nothing 'bouncy' about resilience. Instead, it is the ability to keep plodding on and deal with challenges when they arise. This doesn't mean a child will not feel the pain of the challenge at hand. In fact, it is important they know they are allowed to feel the pain of defeat or the trials and tribulations they face. Instead, resilience is about having the capacity and skills needed to recover from these difficulties.

🦉 A Word to the Wise

In the early 1990s, scientists in Oracle, Arizona, developed a centre for research, teaching, and lifelong learning about the earth and its living systems called *Biosphere 2*. A huge glass dome was created to house an artificially controlled environment with purified air and water, healthy soil, and filtered light. To this day, it remains the largest closed ecological system ever created. The intention was to create perfect growing conditions for trees, fruits, and vegetables. The experiment initially went well, with one exception. The scientists discovered that when they grew trees within the Biosphere, they fell over before fully matured. Initially, this baffled the researchers until they eventually realised that the dome lacked wind, which provided the stress to ensure the trees grew strong enough to support themselves. As the wind blows on trees, it causes their root systems to grow deeper, and this supports the tree as it grows taller. The same could be argued for our children. Minor stressors build strength. Importantly, I said minor, not major.

As our children overcome minor challenges, they realise they are strong and resilient. They can survive and thrive. Instead of shielding them from every struggle, we can help them realise, in very low-stakes situations, that they can face life's challenges. I am not saying to subject them to a hurricane, but if we over-protect them and shelter them from every little breeze, they will never realise they can face the storms that life throws at them.

As the old English proverb says, when the caterpillar thought the world was over, it became a butterfly. If our children face their own challenges, they are more likely to cope with difficulties in adulthood. Instead of smoothing every path for them, we can show them that they are strong and capable, and we have every confidence in them.

⊕ What Does the Research Say?

Dr Joan Rosenberg, author of *90 Seconds to a Life You Love*, is a psychologist who specialises in resilience. She talks about the importance of being able to sit with emotions. She describes feelings as a form of energy. They operate like waves on a shoreline. The energy from the wave pushes it up onto the shoreline for a short period, but then the energy dissipates and the wave retreats. Emotions operate the same way, she argues. Generally, they don't last more than 90 seconds, and if we can ride the wave of emotion, we become more resilient. Feelings are transient. They come and go. Knowing that most tricky feelings are short-lived, and what makes them linger is our own self-criticism or negative self-talk, can help us to have the courage to sit with them. She reminds us not to label some feelings or emotions as negative for our children. Instead, we should refer to them as challenging (or for little ones, we often say these feelings are 'tricky'). She argues that if we can slow down and take deep breaths until the rush of biochemicals dissipates (about 90 seconds later), it will help us to sit with the feeling and allow it to pass. The lesson for us as parents is that as much as we may want to try to rescue our children from the wave, they will develop resilience if we can instead support them to withstand it.

One of the problems in doing the above is the pain it causes us to watch our child struggle with strong emotions. For most of us, the overwhelming emotion we experience when we see our children struggling is the need to reassure, protect, or jump in and rescue them.

From The Horse's Mouth

If you are anything like me, you may well be a 'Little Miss Fix-It' when it comes to your children. If my children are in pain, if they are struggling or facing challenges, I find a huge temptation to jump in and try to fix it. I must make a conscious effort to step back from the child and let them take control. Although in the past, fixing things made me feel needed, like I was making a difference and being a 'good parent,' I was, in fact, not helping my children. Letting our children go through their struggles while knowing that we are there as a listening ear in the background, if necessary, is empowering.

What strategies can we use to help our children thrive? We can start with connection, which gives children a sense of belonging. Then, we want to support a belief in their abilities and a feeling of self-worth. Feelings of competence and a belief that they can control outcomes are all important. Let's look at how we can help to develop these competencies within our children. But first, let's love them.

It Starts with Love

Before we look at all the ways we can support our children's self-worth, coping skills, and feelings of strength and capability, let's start from a position of love. You may have heard of filling a child's love cup. The idea is that every child has a cup that needs to be filled with love, affection, and time. Their love cup holds their emotional fuel. Meeting their need for connection by filling their love cup is as important as meeting their need for food and rest. Most challenging behaviours happen when their love cup is running low. The demands of life can empty their cup, including meeting the expectations of school or society, loneliness or isolation, and difficulties with friendships or siblings. All these challenges can empty their cup. However, we can refill their cup by spending time with them doing something they love, listening to them, and playing.

Resilience and self-esteem are very closely linked, and both involve knowing that I am loved and knowing that I am strong and capable. Our connection with our children is all-important in developing these skills and dispositions. Taking the time to develop responsive relationships and making our home a place of love and affection will help our children to blossom. People and our connection to them bring real meaning into our lives. Children develop within relationships, and their most important relationships are those with their family and primary carers.

☼ Give It a Try!

There are three times in the day when it is recommended that we focus on connecting with our children. These are all points of transition, known to be moments where connection is all important. They are:

On waking in the morning:
Our first interactions with our children set the day's tone. Using these moments to focus on a calm and positive connection soothes our children into the day. This could be anything from putting their school uniform on the radiator so that it is warm on a winter's morning to preparing a favourite breakfast to a

'routine' greeting – 'Morning gorgeous girl.' We can build positive connections with just a smile or a hug.

After separation:

Reconnection after separation during preschool or school is a great time for forging family bonds. Once again, small everyday routines and rituals can bring a sense of calm. Anything from a secret handshake to snuggles on the sofa or asking about the best part of their day can re-establish our connection.

Bedtime:

Bedtime is probably the most common point of connection for parents and their children. This final transition of the day is again a very important opportunity to have one last focus on connection before sleep. Anything from reading bedtime stories, doing belly breathing together, or spending time talking about three things you are grateful for that day can all help to bring us together as one again.

Another effective way to improve connection with our children is by giving hugs. American family therapist Virginia Satir was known for arguing that we can never have enough hugs. She recommended four hugs a day for survival, eight for maintenance, and twelve hugs a day for growth. The research backs her up, showing that hugging has a very positive impact on our bodies and minds. We know that they reduce levels of cortisol, the stress hormone. They also boost our children's dopamine and serotonin levels. Dopamine is known as the pleasure hormone, as it is released when we are doing something that makes us feel good. It is a temporary feeling of reward. When we feel the rush of dopamine in our bodies, we crave it again, and we feel motivated to engage in this way another time so it can be addictive. Serotonin is another 'feel good' chemical within the body.

It helps to control mood, among other things. Low levels of serotonin can negatively impact mood and sleep. Both these chemicals create feelings of happiness and wellbeing. Hugs can also help our children to feel safe and secure.

We now know that the length of a hug matters, too. The average hug lasts about three seconds. However, hugging for twenty seconds has been shown to decrease stress levels. These longer hugs result in greater connection and help to increase the 'love hormone' oxytocin. We know levels of oxytocin rise with physical touch and can result in feelings of happiness and better mood. It is also associated with a decrease in heart rate and blood pressure, so hugging can make us less susceptible to heart disease. It seems that hugs have the power to heal in many ways.

From the Horse's Mouth

What if you are not a natural hugger? When my children were little, I kissed and hugged them all the time, but as they became older, I found I was doing this less and less. My eldest is an absolute hugger, and she taught me that no matter how old your children are, you should continue with those hugs. But even if you or your child are not huggers, you can try other ways to physically connect with them. From touching their shoulders, holding hands, or linking arms with them as you walk, we know that any form of physical touch can be beneficial. But if you start to hug your children on a regular basis, soon you will find that it is not them asking you for hugs, but you are asking for them yourself.

Starting with a focus on love and affection puts us in the perfect position to support our children to fly.

Scaffolding Our Children

We know that when our children are born, they are completely dependent on us as parents to take care of them. As children grow, it is important to gradually remove the supports and allow them to become more independent. One way we can do this is to scaffold our children's learning. Psychologists have long argued that acting in this way is all-important to their independence.

The concept of scaffolding children's learning is an important part of the classroom. The term is linked to the work of Russian Psychologist Lev Vygotsky and his theory on children's cognitive development. He proposes that children are active learners and develop through social interaction with others, particularly those who are more knowledgeable than they are. As scaffolding is used on a building to support it during construction, our support needs to be withdrawn as our child grows more independent. We are there to support and guide, but our role is to assist only when needed. As they progress and become more independent, we adjust the level of support required to encourage our children's confidence.

In this way, we can help our children achieve tasks they would not be able to achieve alone, building their independence as we go. Parents can also foster learning by delivering opportunities that provide these challenges for the child while using guided instruction to support their development. This concept can help us think about what our children can achieve at present and very gently push them out of their comfort zones with minimum support to achieve greater things.

I often say to parents the easiest way to think of scaffolding your children is to see yourself as the clue to the crossword. You are not telling the child the answer, but instead, you are giving them a clue. You want to support them until they reach the point where they feel more confident in their own ability. But remember, once they are at a point of competence and independence, you can step back.

If necessary, you can still dip in and out, offering support. But we want our children to learn to take on tasks themselves, having faith in their ability to overcome any difficulties they face. We also want them to know that we believe they are strong and capable enough to deal with life's challenges. As they get older, they will need to call on us less and less while also knowing that we are there to call on for support if necessary. Very often, it is us, not them, who struggle when the scaffolding comes down completely. We may have to remind ourselves that it was never meant to be there permanently and take pride in the strong and capable young person our child has become.

We would love to give our children a world in which every child can thrive and grow. Indeed, we all are responsible for trying to make the world a better place for our children. But in modern times, we also have a responsibility to support our children in developing the resilience and skill sets that will enable them to cope with the challenges that life will throw at them.

Time To Play

Play is so important to child development that it is recognised by the United Nations High Commission on Human Rights as a fundamental right of every child. Yet, while experts across the world recognise it as an essential component of healthy development, the time children spend playing each day has decreased over recent years. We also know that in the past few decades, children's time spent outdoors in free, unstructured play has fallen by fifty per cent. Indeed, children today play eight hours less each week than their counterparts did two decades ago[37]. Issues such as adult concerns about safety, increased screen time, and a more academic focus in childhood are among the reasons why our children have less time for this type of play. The American Academy of Paediatrics has encouraged paediatricians to 'prescribe' play to parents, reminding them that play is a key aspect of childhood.

In education, we know that adult-guided and child-directed play are both important for a child's development. But, particularly during the early years, most of a child's development happens during unstructured play, so the importance of free play cannot be underestimated. It is the primary way in which children learn to solve problems, engage in conflict resolution, and become emotionally resilient. Free play enhances cognitive flexibility, brain functioning, and executive control. It helps develop self-regulation, collaboration, and the ability to reason about hypothetical events. Play helps regulate the body's stress response through joyfulness and shared communication. So, it is very worrying that today, our children are often deprived of freedom for exploration.

Learning From Psychology

We know that children engage in many types of free play, each involving different developmental benefits. Such as:

Object Play:
This play starts with an infant putting everything into their mouth and later using objects as toys, learning about themselves and their environment. As the child grows, their engagement in object play develops in complexity.

Pretend Play:
This play allows children to experiment with taking on roles. These play experiences help children learn about their likes and dislikes, interests, and abilities. They experiment with role-playing to make sense of what they have observed in the real world.

Rough-and-Tumble Play:
Akin to the play seen in animals, this play enables children to take risks in a relatively safe environment. Studies have also shown

that rough-and-tumble play helps children learn to regulate, understand, and manage their emotions.

Outdoor Play:
Playing outdoors allows children to integrate different senses and use their bodies and minds in tandem. Outdoor play tests their abilities and helps them develop new skills through trial and error. Research shows more outdoor play in schools results in greater academic success.

There are many benefits of free play, where the child has control, can create their own rules, and establish their own limits. Research has found that this type of play can support child development in many ways. Physically, it helps to build strength and coordination and develops spatial understanding. Emotionally, it helps cultivate imagination and creativity and supports self-esteem and self-regulation. It allows children to understand, manage, and express their emotions. As children communicate and collaborate in play, it helps them understand other people's perspectives as they share ideas and build empathy. Cognitively, it enhances problem-solving and decision-making skills. It assists children in developing flexible thinking as they tackle complex problems through play.

👍 Give It a Try!

Pam Leo, author of *Connection Parenting*,[38] recommends having ten minutes a day of one-on-one 'special time' spent in play with each of our children. Her preference is rough-and-tumble and physically active play that causes giggles and laughter, which she argues is essential in strengthening family bonds. She believes that children use up their emotional fuel just getting through the day, and as adults, it is important that we help them to refuel. She acknowledges that in today's busy world, it can be challenging to schedule even ten minutes of special time every day with each of our children, but she recommends planning for this to make sure it happens. This might involve some flexibility, maybe staggering bedtimes, making trade-offs with your partner timewise, or enlisting the support of other family members.

How we connect with each of our children will depend on their age and personalities. But the more effort we put into achieving these ten minutes spent in connection every day, the more our relationship with our child will blossom. Think of it as 'pockets of presence.' These are pockets of time when we really connect with our child.

As well as time spent in play together, it is important also to provide opportunities for free play with peers. We know that this type of play has many benefits. It involves greater levels of creativity and imagination than solo play, providing opportunities for interaction with others. It supports problem-solving and decision-making skills and helps support the important skills of self-regulation and conflict resolution. These are skills which can be difficult to sit and 'teach' to children. They are best developed through active learning, where the child is engaged socially with peers, and learning comes naturally through play. So, if you tend to schedule a lot of your children's free time and find yourself running from activity to activity, consider reducing planned activities and giving more time to free play.

When I think of my childhood experiences of play, we had more of a free-range childhood than today's children. We were told to 'get out and play' if we announced that we were bored! We played out on the road almost every day after school until dark. We had time to explore, time to daydream, time to be bored, and time to figure out how to overcome boredom. We had time to get ourselves into trouble and think about how to get ourselves out of it. We were given greater freedom than children today, allowing us to develop social and emotional skills that can only be learned through experience.

Today, our children attend many extra-curricular activities and spend additional time in the car rushing between various activities. So, while children in the past had few daily transitions, children today have many. We know that transitions are a point of conflict for children and the adults who care for them. Indeed, in educational settings, we constantly strive to reduce the number of transitions children experience in a day for this exact reason. It can be worth considering if an over-scheduled life is contributing to a child's anxiety.

From riding their bikes, playing make-believe or dress-up, sand and water play, block play and construction play, child-led artwork, or outdoor activities such as running, swinging, or climbing, each has value for your child's development. Never believe they are 'just playing.' They are building their bodies and brains.

Healthy Risk-Taking

We often think as parents that our job is that of a protector with the goal of keeping our children safe all the time. Yes, safety is important. But our role is also to support our children in becoming strong and independent, so they learn to do things themselves as they grow stronger. Healthy risk-taking is one way we can support our children to become aware of just how capable they are.

In her book *It's OK to Go Up the Slide*, Educationalist Heather Shumaker asks why children try to go up the slide in playgrounds[39]. She advises that they do this because they seek risk and challenge in their play. Going up the slide is not only fun but also a healthy adventure that helps children feel powerful in their play. She argues that going up the slide helps them to test their strength and find their limits. This is just one way our children seek out excitement and fun, but, as parents, we often limit that sense of adventure. It could be argued that in modern society, we underestimate the ability of our children to cope with risk while also tending to overestimate the dangers in the world. This leads us to overprotect children from possible dangers in risky play, which is very different from past generations when children were allowed to play more freely. The danger is that depriving children of opportunities for risk-taking means depriving them of opportunities to test their boundaries and learn how strong and capable they are.

So, what does risky play involve? There are six categories of play that are included under the risky play umbrella. These are:

Playing at height, which includes opportunities to climb, balance, hang, or swing from heights. Often, children take some time deciding whether to jump from heights, which shows us that they are making choices about the level of risk that feels safe to them.

Playing at speed, which can often involve swings, bikes, or scooters. The unpredictability and thrill of this play, involving an element of being scared by the speed, seems to be what children enjoy.

Rough-and-tumble play involves wrestling, play fighting, chasing, and 'pretend' sword fighting. This is one which many adults are often nervous about. We know from research that young mammals engage in this type of play, too, and there seem to be unwritten rules, almost a code of conduct, about levels of aggression whereby younger children are accommodated. Injury in this type of play usually occurs by accident rather than intent.

Next, we have using dangerous tools. Adults usually supervise this type of play, which includes playing with ropes, knives, saws, and various power tools. You will often find children engrossed in this play, deep in concentration, suggesting that they have been prepared by adults with discussion about the level of risk and are aware of being careful.

Then, we have engaging with natural elements, which involves playing with elements such as fire, cold, or moving water. Again, this type of play is usually engaged in with adult supervision.

Finally, we have play where children 'disappear' or get lost, which involves exploring new places or spaces, either alone or in groups.

Most children love to hide from adults from the earliest experience of 'peek-a-boo.' This leads to playing in spaces where they feel that adults cannot see them. This play often involves loose parts such as sheets, wood, or boxes, with which the children can make dens or hiding places.

All the above results in the child experiencing exhilaration and an element of fear and involves a certain level of risk. However, they also lead to feelings of pride and accomplishment, resulting in the child seeing themselves as a strong and capable participant in play. As adults, our role is to assess the level of risk involved and consider the possible steps that will enable the child to play in this way while achieving a balance between safety and possible risk. Ask yourself, what is the worst that can happen? If they are walking on a beam in the gym, they may fall off and graze their knees, but is that worth the learning and feeling of accomplishment as they gain their balance?

The idea of safe risk-taking is not to leave children exposed to danger. In fact, the adult plays an important role in ensuring that children have the freedom and opportunities for risky play within a framework of safety. This might involve setting boundaries, outlining safety rules to follow, and ensuring that the activities are considered from a risk-benefit perspective. It also often involves giving children the time and resources to try things that challenge them without adults constantly intervening.

☝ Give it a Try!

Here are some ideas for 'safe risk-taking' activities for children:

Playing at Height:
Climbing frames, slides, and playground equipment that involve jumping, balancing, and hanging. Climbing trees and hills.

Playing at Speed:
Spinning, skating, sliding, and riding bikes and scooters at rapid speed. Using slopes and ramps to travel at speed.

Rough and Tumble:
Play fighting, pretend sword fighting, chasing games, spinning and dancing, rolling down hills, using imaginary weapons or items like 'light sabers.'

Playing with Natural Elements:
This usually involves playing with water and fire. It can include play in mud kitchens and forest school type activities, such as camping activities involving lighting fires (under adult supervision) and cooking involving using the hob.

Using Real-Life Tools:
Using hammers, nails, screwdrivers, and drills in outdoor activities. Cooking activities involving peeling and cutting with knives. (When using real-life tools, it is always necessary to conduct a 'step by step' instruction programme and include safety equipment such as goggles as they may be needed, with adult supervision recommended.)

Disappearing Type Play:
Building forts and dens, playing hide and seek, playing in wooded areas, using tents and camouflage to hide.

A study of children's play conducted by the University of Exeter found that when children spent more time playing outdoors and adventurously, they had lower levels of anxiety[40]. Importantly, they also found that children with more opportunities to play adventurously before the Pandemic displayed more positive moods during the initial lockdown periods. The findings suggest that these experiences allowed those children to be braver in difficult circumstances. We know that children learn to tolerate uncertainty when exposed to uncertainty. This play brings uncertainty, the need to evaluate risk, and feeling nervous in a positive context. In terms of physiological arousal (heart beating, butterflies in their tummy) they are experiencing these 'symptoms' of anxiety in fun situations (maybe riding their bike very fast). The child learns they can cope with these slightly anxiety-provoking situations, which helps them build confidence in the world and their abilities.

One thing to be aware of when we encourage children to have a go at something new is the language we use. We often say, 'Be careful,' but this does not teach our children how to safely take risks. It is not specific enough to be helpful and only gives our child the message that there is something to be fearful of. If you are a parent who, like me, can overuse the term 'be careful,' try to think of some alternatives you might use. You can talk through safety before your child starts an activity, preferably asking questions so they are thinking about how to respond to potential risks. For example, saying something like 'What's your plan for climbing that tree?' or 'How are you planning to get down?' encourages the child to think through their plans rather than just telling them what to do.

The message is to watch the language you use when your child is engaging in any activity that is challenging them. Positive language can encourage them to have a 'give it a go' mentality. For example:

Instead of 'Be careful,' these are some ideas you might try:

- Try… using your arms, moving your feet/arms slowly.
- Do you feel… secure on that branch/stable on that log?
- How will you… reach the edge/get across the gap/get down?
- Notice… those slippery rocks/the shaky branch/how deep it is.
- Are you feeling… scared/safe/in control?

You can also use phrases like 'Keep going, you can do it,' or 'Can you reach a little further?' or 'You can use your arms to balance,' encouraging an awareness of what their bodies are capable of. If they struggle to know what to do next, ask them, 'Do you have a plan?' to encourage them to think through their options. Or, if needed, say, 'Let me know if you need any help.' But remember, if you feel your child can navigate the situation themselves, say nothing.

If we can overcome our fears and show confidence in our children, it can have such an impact on their self-belief and feelings of capability. We hope to then find a child who has the confidence to make their own choices, take on their own challenges, and embrace autonomy.

From the Horse's Mouth

When my children were young, I thought my role was that of protector. My job was to always keep them safe. But I have moved away from that belief and now see myself in the role of supporter. Instead of constantly trying to shield my children from all pain, I want them to believe that they are strong and capable enough to handle what life might throw at them. Instead of keeping them away from all potential harm, I have learned that those small emotional bruises from minor failures teach them that they are strong and resilient.

If we want them to grow into strong, capable adults, we need to give them the space for safe risk-taking. If we can provide them with the freedom to take risks, make choices, and build resilience, they will no longer look over their shoulder for our support but instead forge ahead with autonomy. It is not about getting it right all the time. It is about learning not to be afraid to give things a try.

Locus of Control

Another important idea to consider when looking at resilience is a concept developed by Julian Rotter when he considered children's attitudes towards problem-solving[41]. His investigation led him to consider children's beliefs about control as internal or external. Rotter developed a questionnaire called *The Internal–External Locus of Control Scale,* used as the standard measure to evaluate an individual's sense of personal control. The questionnaire contains twenty-nine pairs of statements. One statement in each pair represents a belief in an internal locus of control (a sense of individual autonomy), and the second represents an external locus of control (circumstances external to the individual). For each pair, the test subject must select the statement they agree with the most. Two examples of pairs of statements are:

- **1a.** Getting a good job depends on being in the right place at the right time.
- **1b.** Becoming a success is a matter of hard work. Luck has little to do with it.

- **2a.** Sometimes, I can't understand how teachers arrive at the grades they give.
- **2b.** There is a connection between how hard I study and the grades I get.

In the above cases, the first statement represents an external locus of control, and the second represents an internal locus of control.

Children with an internal locus of control believe they have the capability within them to deal with problems they face. They believe they have a degree of autonomy over their world and can work towards solving difficult problems. However, those with an external locus of control are more likely to believe that the challenges they face are outside their control, perhaps influenced by luck or chance, but, importantly, not within their control. These children are more likely to believe they need others to step in and deal with difficult situations on their behalf.

We know that having an internal locus of control impacts our motivation and potential for success. It has been shown to impact psychological wellbeing and future life satisfaction. It is not surprising that children and young people who believe they have some control over their lives are more likely to put effort into tasks, persevere with challenges, and, as adults, report greater work satisfaction.

Interestingly, over the past five decades, there have been great changes in the number of children and teens with a more external focus. Research on five decades of American students[42] found that our teens increasingly believe their lives are controlled by outside forces. Locus of control has become substantially more external from the 1960s until the 2000s, with the average college student in 2002 having a more external locus of control than eighty per cent of college students in the 1960s. It is argued that there is a connection between this rise in external locus of control and the increase in anxiety and depression reported in American teens during the same period. When a child or young adult believes they have no control over their lives, it is not surprising that they are more likely to become anxious.

One important thing for parents to know about locus of control is that it is not set in stone. We can help our children develop a more internal locus of control by giving them as much control over their lives as possible.

With little ones, we usually start with controlled choices, meaning we give them two or three options. The easiest way to do this involves decisions about people, clothes, and food. These choices help to set the foundation for a feeling of control over their lives.

☝ Give it a Try!

Here are some ideas for controlled choices you can give to young children:

- As you prepare for preschool, ask what they think would be best for the weather today: their shorts or tracksuit bottoms. Will they wear a T-shirt, or is it cold enough to need a sweatshirt? Do they need their welly boots today, or would their trainers be OK for the weather?
- Would they prefer cheese and crackers or a bread roll for their snack? Would they like peas, broccoli, or carrots with their dinner? Would they like an apple or an orange after dinner?
- When going to bed at night, ask if they would like to have their bath before or after supper. Would they like Mum or Dad to read their bedtime story tonight? Would they like to read a second story tonight or listen to a mindfulness app?

As they get older, move towards more age-appropriate options. You can expand the number of choices and teach them that once they have made the decision, they must stick to it. Talk to them about the consequences of their choices and evaluate the impact of their decisions after the event.

Giving them controlled choices gives our children good foundations for decision-making. It helps them understand that they have control over their lives and autonomy over their worlds. As your child gets older, continue to involve them in decisions about their everyday lives, giving them choices that help them develop confidence in their ability to make good decisions.

Problem-Solving

When there is a challenge at hand, the skill of problem-solving will go a long way to take back control from anxious feelings. The most important way we can support our children in becoming confident problem solvers is not to solve all their problems for them. As loving parents, we often jump in and try to 'fix' any issues our children experience. We know we have better-developed problem-solving skills than they have, so the temptation is to protect them whenever we feel they are at risk. We want them to learn that when things go wrong, they can cope. They need to learn this and practise it for themselves.

How can we help? When a problem arises, discuss options. We want our children to come to understand there are always options. Help them to brainstorm ideas and support them in making choices. If we break down the steps involved in problem-solving, they are:

- Identifying the exact problem.
- Brainstorming as many solutions as possible.
- Evaluate the consequences of each of these possible actions.
- Choosing the best option.
- Give that option a try.
- Consider how it went.

If your child has been used to you jumping in and 'fixing' their problems for them, they might struggle to come up with solutions to problems. Encourage them to think of ideas, no matter how crazy they might sound. Don't dismiss any ideas they come up with, even if that idea is for you to 'fix' it for them (which you have no intention of doing!). You want them to learn the skill of brainstorming. You want them to come up with as many ideas as they can. If they are struggling, you can offer some help but try to wait until they have attempted to find some ideas themselves. Yours should only add to the brainstorm.

Again, when choosing the best option, it is important to stand back and let them take control. If they select an option that involves you fixing the problem for them, at this stage of evaluation, you can explain that you cannot do that and rule that option out. Once they choose the most comfortable option, stand back and let them try it out. I know this can be very hard to do when that is not the solution you would have liked them to choose. If they choose a solution that may have a minor negative impact, for example, if they have had a fight with a friend in school, and their solution is to tell the teacher, you might gently ask them to consider the impact of that option again. But you want your child to learn to make decisions for themselves, and sometimes that involves letting them try solutions that would not be your choice (unless their solution could cause significant distress to your child). Having a go at picking a potential solution in a low-stakes situation is a great learning opportunity for your child.

☝ Give it a Try!

Introducing young children to the basics of problem-solving:

- Listen while the child explains the problem.
- Repeat it back to the child to make sure you have understood correctly.
- Ask the child to identify any possible solutions. Remember, they don't have to be perfect solutions. Every idea is a possibility.
- If necessary, expand on these solutions with some ideas of your own. You want them to see there are always many options.
- Reflect with the child all the possible solutions, evaluate the possible positive or negative outcomes and narrow them down.
- Allow the child to choose the solution they want to try.

After the child has tried out their chosen solution, sit with them and review how it went. How did their solution work out? In hindsight, would they still choose that option? Would one of the other options have been more effective? What have they learned from the experience? Remember, your child is learning that even if the solution does not work out as planned, they can survive these low-stakes difficulties. But please make sure to finish with a reminder that you are so proud of them for working through the problem-solving process and taking on the challenge of overcoming that problem themselves.

Going through this problem-solving process is helping your child develop the building blocks for good decision-making when they are older. You want them to get used to considering different options when faced with a problem rather than feeling helpless and needing help from others.

If our children see problems as external to them, then they can work on developing strategies to solve the issue. Too often, our children generalise about themselves when faced with difficulties. Viewing a challenge as a problem that can be solved with various strategies moves the focus to an external problem rather than something within the child.

Hope and Mindset

How our children explain life events to themselves can impact their lives in many ways. Psychologists talk about attributional styles when they look at children's ways of thinking. These styles refer to how the child uses information to form a causal explanation for events that take place in their lives.

Martin Seligman, considered one of the founding fathers of positive psychology, has conducted a lot of research in this area. Seligman and colleagues use the three Ps to explain the three dimensions that influence how we form explanations. These are *Personalisation* (namely internality versus externality – whether we see the explanation as lying within ourselves or external to ourselves), *Permanence* (stability versus instability, whether we see explanations as stable over time or temporary), and *Pervasiveness* (whether we see explanations as global, applying to many domains, or specifically limited to one area). For example, say your child struggles with their tables test in school on a Friday. If they have a pessimistic attributional style, their thinking after the test might be:

- 'I am no good at tables.' - They are *internalising* the situation – linking it to their ability.
- 'I am going to fail all my tables tests.' - Their thinking is *stable*. They believe the situation will keep happening.
- 'I am going to do so badly at school because I am stupid.' - They are *globalising*. They feel this difficulty applies to all situations.

The above response would be considered a negative attributional style.

However, some children have a more positive attributional style. In this case, the child might say:

- 'Those tables were so difficult.' - They are *externalising* the situation – it's not me, it was just a hard test.
- 'If I work harder, I will do better next time.' - The situation is *temporary*. It can change over time.
- 'I failed that test because it was so hard.' - The situation is *localised*. It relates to that test but not necessarily to other situations or their overall ability.

The attributional styles outlined above can help us consider how our children view the world. They are not fixed in place. We can learn to change and adapt. Focusing our awareness on the explanations our children give for events in their lives can shed light on their ways of thinking. Research on attributional styles has found that if we have a positive approach, we are more likely to use active problem-solving techniques when faced with challenges. Our child is more likely to think, 'I need to consider what strategies I might use to deal with this problem.' If they have a more negative attributional style, they are more likely to use avoidance strategies, such as giving up when faced with life's challenges. This suggests that their attributional style impacts not only their feelings but also their actions.

Hope is important in developing resilience and relates to locus of control and problem-solving. You might think hopefulness is just wishing it will be, but no, it is a way of thinking. Hope is a belief that when times are tough, we can make them better. It is the thing that keeps us going when faced with challenges. Psychologists suggest there are three things that make up hopeful thinking. Approaching life in a goal-oriented way, planning different pathways to reach the goal, and a belief in agency, the ability to plan and adapt to achieve the goal. The suggestion is that those who engage in hopeful thinking can establish clear goals, consider how they might achieve them, and stick to their task even in the face of challenges.

Importantly, hopeful thinking is something our children can learn. It is clear that children with an internal locus of control and experience and support in problem-solving will feel greater levels of agency and, therefore, should be more hopeful when facing life's challenges.

·Ṽ· Top Tip!

Using a mantra while getting ready to start their day can help your child build a more hopeful perspective and find their inner bravery. Here are some ideas for morning mantras your child might like to use. Look at these ideas together and let them choose their favourite or make one of their own. They can change mantras as they face different challenges during the year.

Ideas for mantras:

- I am strong and brave.
- I am a good problem-solver.
- I am a good learner.
- I am kind and think of others.
- I can do great things.

At the end of each day, the child can think back on their mantra and see if they achieved it or if it is something they might like to keep working on.

The idea of hope is closely linked to the concept of a growth mindset. This idea comes from the work of Carol Dweck of Stanford University. She researched students' attitudes towards educational failure and discovered that the students fell into two general categories. The first she calls a *fixed mindset*. These children believe that their intelligence is fixed or set in stone. They think that it is our natural ability or talent which brings success. They also tend to avoid challenges they feel they cannot easily achieve. However, those with a growth mindset believe intelligence and ability can grow with effort. They think we grow and change as we work hard to achieve tasks. They are more likely to see mistakes as a part of learning and will put in time and effort to learn new things. She argues that most children have a general tendency towards one mindset or another. Without intervention, mindsets are relatively stable. But we can teach them.

Learning From Psychology

One study by Dweck[43] divided seventh graders into two groups, each of which took part in a different workshop on the brain. The first group were taught about the different stages of memory.

The second group was taught about the brain's plasticity – its potential to change and adapt as we learn. They explained to this group that the brain, like a muscle, grows stronger through use. The students in this workshop, which explained how intelligence could be developed, were more likely to report after the session that working hard was necessary to achieve. Three times as many students in this group showed an increase in effort and motivation than the fixed mindset group, impacting their academic performance. Nearly two years later, they were still outperforming the group with a more fixed theory of intelligence.

So, how can we support our children in developing a growth mindset? Teach your child about how their brain works. Once children understand that the brain grows new connections as they practise how to do something, they are more open to learning new things. We can do this by encouraging them to use the word *yet*. When they tell you they can't do something, when they tell you they don't understand something, when they tell you that something they tried didn't work, add the word *yet* to the end of their sentence. You can't do it *yet*. You don't understand it *yet*. It didn't work *yet*. It doesn't make sense *yet*. Our children need to learn to embrace the word *yet*.

Follow-up research on growth mindset argues that we should encourage our children to take a strategic approach. Simply telling yourself to try harder could become discouraging if you use an unproductive strategy. Instead, being strategic might motivate you to search for new strategies, consult with mentors, or seek other experts. We need to encourage our children to self-monitor to seek out better strategies when things go wrong. So, when effort doesn't seem to have the results we hoped for, we need to be strategic in our thinking.

Those with a strategic mindset tend to ask themselves strategy-eliciting questions such as:

- What can I do to help myself?
- How else can I do this?
- Is there a way to do this even better?

These are three questions we can encourage our children to ask themselves when working on challenges.

The danger of the word *should* is closely linked to the concept of a growth mindset. A minor change in thinking can help with this. When faced with a problem, we often start to think about what we *should* do to solve it. Instead, try to reframe it as thinking about what we *could* do.

Trying to solve problems considering what we *should* do tricks our minds and narrows our focus into searching for one solution. Whereas, changing our language and considering what we *could* do opens our minds to looking for multiple possibilities. We are more likely to consider a wider range of more imaginative solutions.

A Word to the Wise

Consider the example of US Airways Captain Chelsey 'Sully' Sullenberger, who became an overnight hero when he safely landed in the Hudson River after an unlucky encounter with a flock of geese in 2009. All 155 passengers and crew aboard survived. Shortly after taking off, his plane lost both engines, and he had to make an emergency decision about what to do. The 'what *should* I do' response was to try to land at the nearest airport runway. He considered this option but knew it was flawed. Instead, he allowed himself to think about what he *could* do. Having considered various options, he chose to land the plane on the Hudson River, saving the lives of all aboard. The point is he did not allow himself to be constrained by the textbook response but considered all possible options. This is the thinking we want to encourage in our children. The hope is that this approach becomes a learned behaviour, and when they are older, this will be their go-to method for decision-making.

The problem with the word should is that it suggests there is a right and a wrong way of living our lives, a right and a wrong way of interacting in the world, and a right and wrong way of being. The word can be very limiting, making our children feel inadequate and see themselves as failing. I *should* be top of the class. I *should* have a wide friendship group. I *should* be thin. Developing an awareness of your child's language will help you speak to them about issues like this.

Emotion Coaching

One of the important learning experiences in childhood is developing an emotional vocabulary. Having the words to describe their feelings does not always come naturally to our children. Taking the time to help our children develop an emotional vocabulary from a young age helps them to express their emotions verbally. We can do this in many ways, starting with ourselves. We can remember to not only use the umbrella term for how we are feeling but instead to use a wider range of emotions to express our feelings. For example, are you feeling sad, or if you consider the emotion more deeply, are you feeling disappointed, tearful, or indeed hurt? Are you feeling anxious, or are you feeling stressed, nervous, or vulnerable? Are you feeling happy, or are you thankful, excited, or joyful? We often have a 'go-to' expression that we use to describe general emotions. Taking a bit of time to consider them more deeply allows us to use and model a wider range of vocabulary.

☀ Top Tip!

Paint charts can be a great way to support children in understanding the difference between shades of emotions. The strips of colour in various hues can be used as a visual scale of the strength of emotion. For example, a strip of various yellow colours can be used to describe different levels of happiness. If the strongest yellow colour is at the top of the strip, we can call that colour Ecstatic. Then, the next less vibrant yellow on the strip could be Happy. The next less vibrant colour might be called Content.

Similarly, with a strip of red colours, the most vibrant red at the top of the strip might be called Furious. The next less vibrant red could be called Angry, leading down to the less vibrant, Annoyed. Using these scales can help the child understand and recognise the different intensities of emotion and can help with conversations about managing the various levels of emotions.

As parents, we sometimes say we want our children to be happy. But none of us are permanently happy. Instead, we should support our children in accepting and dealing with the full range of emotions, even the tricky ones.

American Psychologist John Gottman first developed the idea of emotion coaching to tune in to our children's feelings, helping them better understand their emotions and learn to cope with the trickier ones. There are five steps involved in emotion coaching. These are:

- Becoming aware of their emotions.
- Recognising them as an opportunity for teaching.
- Listening empathetically and validating their feelings.
- Helping the child to label their emotions.
- Exploring strategies for coping with the situation.

When a child is scared or anxious, the temptation as a parent can be to persuade them that all is well. This can feel to the child as if we are dismissing their feelings. Instead, the idea of emotion coaching is to acknowledge those feelings.

Over the coming weeks, take any opportunity when your child is facing a tricky emotion or a tricky situation to connect with them and talk about their emotional responses. Show empathy for your child's emotional struggles, but when you are both calm, talk to them about the feelings they experienced. Validate their feelings. This means making clear that it is only natural to experience tricky emotions at times. Help them find the emotional language to express their feelings and, if necessary, go through the problem-solving process above to help them work through how they might deal with that situation in the future.

We all want to support our children to be strong and capable of all we know they can achieve, and a very effective way to do this is to give them the psychological space to come to terms with tricky emotions. Doing this helps children better understand their feelings and helps them sit with the discomfort long enough to come to terms with it. Indeed, the goal is to sit with these emotions long enough to learn how to tackle them.

One of the important steps in emotion coaching is normalising these difficult emotions, which means helping our children to understand that they are not alone in experiencing them. The best way to do that is to let them know you have felt this way, too. Whether it is embarrassment, frustration, jealousy, fear, or guilt, we can share a story with our children about a time when we felt the same way.

☝ Give it a Try!

The way we communicate with our children when they are struggling will either help or hinder their emotional development.

Here are some ways we can speak to our children that will help us (and them) to better understand the needs behind their behaviour:

- Instead of telling your child how you think they feel, question how they may feel. 'It sounds as if you are feeling frustrated/angry/upset ....' Or 'It looks like you are really struggling today. Would you like to tell me how you are feeling?'
- Acknowledge difficulties and try to empathise with the feelings behind them. 'It looked like it was hard for you to wait your turn earlier. That must have felt very frustrating.' Or 'I noticed that your friend was so upset earlier. How did that make you feel?'
- When they do well, give very specific, descriptive praise to acknowledge how well they have done. 'Wow, I noticed you told your little brother to do his breathing when he was feeling frustrated today. It really helped him to calm down.' Or 'I really liked the way you waited your turn for the swings today. I know how hard it can be to wait your turn in the playground.'

Stories are another great way to talk to children about emotions and help them name them. When reading to them, ask them how they think the characters feel. Have they ever felt that way? What could they do if they felt that way again? Give them some ideas and strategies to use.

☼ Give it a Try!

Talking through some ideas about what they can do when dealing with tricky emotions can help prepare them with ideas to support balance when they are feeling big feelings. For example, they might:

- Tell someone how they are feeling.
- Take some deep breaths.
- Count up to, or down from, ten.
- Run, skip, or jump.
- Draw what they are feeling.
- Squeeze a stress ball.
- Do ten jumping jacks.
- Use positive self-talk, 'I can do this,' or 'let it go.'
- Pop bubble wrap.

Remind them that tricky feelings come and go. They are not permanent. Just because you feel angry, jealous, or frustrated right now does not mean that feeling will last. It is normal to feel lots of feelings, but having some ideas on how to handle them when they come can be helpful.

A final thought on the idea of the emotional language we use and the hidden impact it can have concerns the words we use to describe our children, particularly those who struggle with anxiety. Here are some examples of the difference language can make to our beliefs about our children and the labels we use to describe them:

- Instead of fearful, we can describe them as cautious.
- Instead of needy, we can describe them as seeking connection.
- Instead of impulsive, we can describe them as spontaneous.
- Instead of dramatic, we can describe them as passionate.
- Instead of fussy, we can describe them as selective.
- Instead of hyper-vigilant, we can describe them as watchful.

It can be worth taking the time to consider the language we use when talking to or about our children and re-framing your thoughts in a more positive way.

Making Mistakes

If you take my advice and allow your children more control over their own lives, more input into decision-making about their lives, and encourage them in safe risk-taking, won't they make mistakes? Yes, indeed, they will! The thought of our children making mistakes can frighten us so much.

Psychologist Alfred Adler compares life to learning to swim. What happens when we learn to swim? We make mistakes. We then make more mistakes. We continue to make all the mistakes we possibly can, some of them repeatedly. But then, what do we find? That we can swim. He reminds us that life is the same for our children as learning to swim. We should encourage them not to be afraid of making mistakes, for there is no other way to learn how to live. So many of our children see mistakes as failure. It is so important that they change that viewpoint and see mistakes as learning opportunities. When our children make mistakes, they are not failing. They are learning.

Recent neurological research on the brain confirms that mistakes are learning opportunities. In fact, mistakes are times when our brain connections grow[44]. When studying the neural connections in brains, researchers found that electrical signals, called synapses, fire when people make mistakes. A signal is sent to ensure conscious attention is given to the mistake. The brain is challenged to cope with the error, which increases electrical activity and results in growth.

The message is clear. We need to encourage children to think of their brain as something that is strengthened with use. As we try new experiences, some connections are strengthened, and some are eliminated. We can encourage our children to try new things, make mistakes, and try again, knowing that their brains can change and adapt because of these different experiences.

🦉 A Word to the Wise

Sometimes, it can be helpful for our children who worry about mistakes to hear about famous failures. Here are a few examples that remind us that often, very successful people have come from a place of failure:

- *Abert Einstein*, a renowned physicist and mathematician, didn't speak until the age of four and could not speak fluently until the age of nine. He was expelled from school and failed the Swiss Federal Polytechnic school entrance exam. However, he created the beginnings of quantum theory and won a Nobel Prize in 1921.
- Before publishing *Harry Potter*, J K Rowling described herself as a jobless, lone parent who was as poor as it was possible to be in modern Britain. She has said that she was the biggest failure she knew. Twelve major publishing houses rejected her until a small literary house published *Harry Potter* seven years after writing the book. Seven years later, according to Forbes, she was the first author to become a billionaire from her writing.
- *Michael Jordan*, one of the greatest sportsmen of all time, speaks about going home and crying after being rejected for a school basketball team. When asked to describe himself, he advised that he has missed more than 9000 shots in his career, lost 300 games, and 26 times missed a game-winning shot. He argues that it is not his natural talent but years of effort, practise, and failure that have contributed to his overall success.

Mistakes are also an opportunity to let them know that we love them unconditionally. They do not have to be a perfect child. Instead, we love them, imperfections and all.

Why do we, as parents, feel so compelled to share our children's successes with the world, and often on social media, from their first steps to the end-of-term awards to their college results? Yet, we are loath to talk about their failures. Naturally, we share when we are proud of our children's achievements, but could it also be that their achievements validate us as parents? We not only share their moment of glory but also bask in it as validation that we have done a good job. Their failures, however, also reflect on us and our parenting skills. We may tell them that their failures are learning experiences, but by our actions, we show them that we only value success. Our fear that their failures reflect on us and our parenting skills, can result in children who also fear failure. For many of our teenagers today, mistakes are not learning experiences. Mistakes are failures. As parents, we need to think about this message very carefully and repeatedly remind them that mistakes do not define them. Mistakes are often the most important learning experiences of their lives.

What about the mistakes you make yourself? Showing our children, that we all make mistakes but can learn and grow from them is a very important life lesson. When we make mistakes in our parenting, let's remember that it is in the dance between rupture and repair that our children develop lasting, trusting relationships with us. From our mistakes and our repair afterwards, they learn to become resilient in the face of difficulties and develop a solid sense of themselves.

CHAPTER 8

The Wider Picture: Family and Community

You're their person.
When they're scared in the middle of the night.
When they're not feeling well.
When they're consumed by big emotions.
When they're anxious or confused or uncertain.
I know it's overwhelming and exhausting,
and all-consuming. But just remember:
You're their person, and what a beautiful privilege that is.

Krista Ward[45]

Psychology reminds us to view children's development as a complex set of relationships, from those within our immediate environment to the wider circles of influence. Therefore, when considering how to support a child experiencing anxiety, we cannot just look at the child in isolation. Instead, we need to consider the wider context, those who are impacted by and influence our children. Seeing the child as being located within these interconnected systems will help us to consider the value of these interactions.

Impact on Siblings

It is important when considering how to support our children who struggle with anxiety that we don't forget their siblings. We know sibling relationships are usually the longest and most formative of our lives. We don't get to choose our siblings, yet they are the people who know us better than anyone else. They have seen our highs and lows and understand our upbringing in a way that few others do. Siblings bond over the complexity of their family lives and shape each other's lives in many ways.

However, as parents, we sometimes expect sibling relationships to be perfect. Instead, they can be up and down at the best of times, even without the additional pressure of one child struggling with anxiety. Although we often think healthy relationships should be in absolute harmony, this is untrue. We already know that healthy relationships include approximately 30% discord. Human interactions can be complicated and confusing. But this is important to our social and emotional development, as working through the inevitable ups and downs of human connection is the path to stronger relationships. Particularly, if one child is struggling with their wellbeing, it impacts family life for their siblings, too.

One thing that can negatively impact our children's relationships is favouritism. If one or both parents treat a sibling as the favoured child, it can cause conflict and tension within the family. Even young children are quick to pick up on preferential treatment and are attuned to whether this treatment is fair. Fair may be the most important word here. Often, if one child in the family is struggling with anxiety, we may focus our attention on that child. It is important, therefore, that any other children in the family understand that, at times, one sibling might need more time and attention if they are under pressure in some way.

To consider this more deeply, let's consider the difference between treating children equally and fairly. As parents, we often equate being fair with treating our children equally, but this is not the case. Treating children equally does not reflect their individuality. There will be times in each child's life when they need a little extra support, time, or attention. Sometimes, we need to explain this to them directly. To make clear that although we love them equally, we need to treat them fairly. Most importantly, keep the lines of communication open with siblings about why the other child needs support. Remind them that there are times in each family member's life when they might need a little bit of extra care and attention for whatever reason.

Research has shown that children are usually aware when one sibling is given preferential treatment. For example, they know that younger children are more likely to get preferred maternal attention, as they depend more on adults to care for their needs. However, most children understand that this is sometimes necessary. This reminds us of children's sense of justice. When they understand that we need to look at each child's needs and circumstances, they often accept that fact. It can help to acknowledge that sometimes it can feel unfair if one child seems to be given more attention than the others.

We also need to be aware of always 'tilting' towards the child who is struggling. We can sometimes over-protect the child we feel needs greater support and become more demanding of their sibling(s). It is also important to ensure that we try to give the sibling who does not need additional support as much attention as possible.

👍 Give it a Try!

Some ideas to support sibling relationships are as follows:

- If you find you are focusing a lot of time and attention on the child who is struggling, try to arrange small amounts of one-on-one time with their sibling. A small amount of quality time will help you to reconnect with them.

- Try to ask your partner or other family members to take up some of the slack if you are spending more time supporting your child who needs extra support.
- Try to create opportunities for connection, arranging family days or trips where both siblings are engaged in something they enjoy doing together.
- Try to make sure that, where possible, appointments for the child who is struggling do not impact the extra-curricular activities of the sibling(s).

If you feel that taking care of your child who is struggling is becoming all-consuming for you, it is very possible that siblings are feeling this pressure too. If they are feeling negative towards their sibling, and to be fair, this is quite natural if a child feels they are not getting the time and attention they need, we can acknowledge those feelings. We do this by listening to their perspective without judgement and perhaps admitting to them that we feel the stress at times as well. It is important they know they can express their honest feelings without feeling shame and that their concerns, whether big or small, are seen and accepted.

It is important also to recognise that the child who struggles with anxiety may feel upset that their siblings do not seem to struggle with their mental health. It can be helpful to let them know that you understand it must be so frustrating to see their siblings seemingly (and remember, just because they 'seem to' does not mean they do) sail through life without any challenges. But we can remind them that anxiety is not who they are. Instead, as they work on their anxiety, they will become stronger and, with your support and backup, reach their full potential.

Friends and Foes

Good friendships can have a huge developmental influence. They benefit both social and emotional development while boosting happiness and wellbeing. This is even more important for children who are already struggling with anxiety. Research shows friendships help our children develop dispositions such as self-esteem and confidence while also assisting them to deal with conflict and adversity. They increase a child's sense of belonging and help them to cope with life's stresses and transitions. Having a hand to hold as you face life's challenges is a great physical and symbolic support. Friendships can be an inoculation against life's difficulties, providing our children with support and comfort in times of trouble.

As children get older, they place a much higher value on emotional closeness with friends, with an emphasis on trust and support within friendships. These relationships help them to learn about themselves, and supportive relationships can foster the skills for healthy adult relationships, such as kindness, empathy, and the ability to listen and console. It can be worth considering in terms of their peer group whether that group provides a supportive environment for your child to grow in. It is important they find friends they can trust, friends who bring out the best in them, and people who like them for who they really are, quirks and all.

🦉 A Word to the Wise

Brené Brown, the Texan researcher and author, speaks about what she calls 'Candle Blower Outers' in our children's lives. She advises us to remind our children that they have an internal flame burning within them. This flame is their spirit, their soul. She reminds us that our children need to surround themselves with people who appreciate their light. And our children want to be the type of friends who, when their friends' lights are shining, tell them that their light is beautiful. They don't, however, want to surround themselves with 'Candle Blower Outers.' They want to make sure to have friends in their lives who appreciate the light within them.

You may have heard the saying that we become the combined average of the five people we are closest to. This is another reminder to be aware of the circle of friends surrounding our children, particularly as they enter the teenage years when friendships play such an important role in terms of influence. Harvard Psychologist David McClelland argues that the people we habitually associate with determine as much as 95% of our success or failure in life. Think about this in terms of our children's inner circle, as they are going to strongly influence their lives and expectations for themselves. Trying to ensure that our children are surrounded by friends who, at best, are actively supportive of them and, at the very least, are a neutral influence on their mental health is something to consider. These friendships can provide a network of support for children in terms of their emotional wellbeing. They can help our children feel a sense of purpose and belonging while reducing feelings of isolation.

One important message for our children is that it is only by being themselves that they will find kindred spirits. As they find friends and lose them, it is important they don't lose themselves. Not everyone will like them. Not everyone will understand them. But the more they can be themselves, the more likely they are to find good friends for life. The ones who understand them, and they understand — the ones who will love them unconditionally.

We cannot choose our children's friendships for them. But encouraging them to have friends from different contexts can be a good idea, so they are not relying on one friend or friendship group but working on developing friendships with different groups. This could be friends from school, friends from their neighbourhood, friends from sports groups, friends from any extra-curricular activities, and cousins as friends. This means that if your child is struggling and friends in one context are not supportive, they have other options in terms of peer support.

If anxiety has been holding your child back in terms of developing a range of friendships, there are two ways you can help to encourage new interactions. The first is to encourage your child to take up a new extra-curricular activity. Clubs or activities provide opportunities for your child to meet peers and engage with them in a structured environment, which they may find easier to negotiate. Whether the activity is sports, the arts, music, photography, or martial arts, it doesn't matter. Any activity that your child enjoys is an opportunity to meet like-minded peers. For a child struggling with anxiety, engaging in a hobby they enjoy often makes it easier for them to interact with peers. The second way to encourage the development of new friendships is to encourage play dates for little ones or games/movie nights in your home for older children. Again, the activity itself is not important. It can be doing anything that your child enjoys. Having children or teens over to your house to engage in an activity that they can all enjoy together gives your child the opportunity to build relationships in a safe space.

Having mentioned the importance of encouraging strong friendships, it is also important to remember that not all our children are social butterflies. Some are happier with a small number of companions. We do not want to put these children under pressure to make new friends. Instead, we can use gentle encouragement to spread their wings. Even one positive relationship can be a protective factor against anxiety.

The Wider Lens

When discussing our children's and teens' relationships with friends and foes, it is worth mentioning social media[46]. We know that social media use among adolescents is almost universal, so it is important to consider if it could be having an impact on levels of anxiety. Currently

YouTube is the most popular platform used by teens, followed by TikTok, Instagram and Snapchat, all three of which are more popular with girls than boys. Despite this widespread use, there are gaps in our understanding of the risks it poses to the mental health of our children.

We know using technology before bedtime can impact sleep. But this is just one issue. Even more important is the content our children are engaging with and its impact on their mental health. Many argue that social media has had a far-reaching effect on our children's experiences, resulting in a move from a more traditional play-based childhood to a more phone-based one. We know this freedom to play and explore is important in overcoming anxiety and building resilience. However, an over-reliance on technology takes up time, which could be spent socialising in person and connecting with others.

Jonathan Haidt and psychologist Jean Twenge have reported a global increase in loneliness among school students, which began in 2012. They advise that this was the year when most students moved from the old-fashioned flip phones to more modern smartphones. It was also the year when Instagram caught fire with teenage girls, and the rise in 'selfie culture' brought with it dangerous levels of visual social comparison. No matter what age we are, engaging in social media usually involves comparing ourselves to others. But particularly in the teenage years, when the brain is very focused on comparison to peers, this can leave our children feeling very inadequate with raised anxiety levels.

For some time now, researchers have been unable to reach an agreement about the impact of social media on our teens. So much of the evidence has shown a relationship between social media and lower mental health, but it has been difficult to prove a causal effect. Most have agreed that this is a very complex issue. However, Jonathan Haidt[47] reports that the most recent investigations which confirm that a reduction of exposure to social media confers benefits, and that exposure to Instagram damages mood and body image, now prove causality. He argues that this research provides direct evidence that social media, and particularly Instagram, negatively impacts the mental health of our teens, particularly our girls.

A study by University College London analysed data from the UK Millenium Cohort Study on 10,904 14-year-olds[48]. They looked at the percentage of adolescents with 'clinically relevant depressive symptoms' by hours of weekday social media use. They found that adolescents with moderate social media use were no more at risk than those with mild social media use. However, there was a clear increase for adolescents with heavy use, and the rate of mood disorders was higher for girls than boys. For boys, moving from two to five hours of daily use was associated with a doubling of depression rates. For girls, it was associated with a tripling of depression rates. They argue that greater social media use is related to online harassment, poor sleep, low self-esteem, and poor body image. These factors, in turn, they argue, relate to higher depressive symptoms.

All the above reminds us of the importance of teaching our teens to think critically when engaging online. We can remind them that everyone online is posting their highlights reel. None of us are truly authentic on social media. It is not possible to fully represent the complexity of a human being online. Social media shows a very one-dimensional story about our lives when we are all more complex, three-dimensional creatures.

Family Connection

We already know that understanding anxiety and how it impacts our bodies and brains is important. But this is important not only for the child experiencing the anxiety and their parents/carers but also for other family members. Anxiety within the family has an impact on every member and can be a cause of distress for not only parents but siblings and extended family members. The better all family members understand the challenges that the child is facing, the better they will be equipped to support that child and you as parents.

Research has shown that we struggle to see the bigger picture when we are stressed. Instead, we focus only on the immediate problem in front of us. We become so focused on our own needs it is difficult to fully appreciate the needs of others. This is an important reminder that the needs of the whole family must be considered. Instead of focusing very much on one child within the family, an emphasis on family bonds can be helpful to everyone in a stressful situation. Even in terms of family conflict resolution or problem-solving, family bonds will make these situations easier to resolve. Maintaining family connections is important in terms of everyone's welfare. Helping your children feel secure and loved in your home will mean that every child, not only the one struggling with anxiety, will gain more confidence in themselves.

It is the quality of our interactions
with our children that is important.
The quiet, in-between moments of family life
are often the ones that children remember long-term.
This is about connection, not perfection.

So, how can we develop a sense of connection within our family? We often think that to create strong family bonds, we need to go on expensive holidays or engage in 'big' activities. It is often the little moments spent together which create the best memories.

From The Horse's Mouth

I remember reading a post on Facebook where a woman advised that one of her favourite memories of childhood was when her mother served up lots of little bits and pieces instead of a normal dinner [Credit: Sarah, Cup of Jo]. In her memory, it was a special treat and something she remembered fondly. When she told her mother about that memory, her mother said she only did that on the evenings when she was so exhausted that she did not have the energy to prepare a full dinner. And yet, these evenings spent with a little picnic dinner of bits and pieces were among her daughter's most treasured memories. I think each of us has memories like this, memories of the simple things that mean so much to us.

This is such a lovely reminder that joy can come in bite-sized pieces. We sometimes tell ourselves that to strengthen family connections, we need to make a meal out of it. But in my view, family connection is borne out of all the little moments, the little bite-size moments of joy. Very often, the little things are the ones we remember.

One reason small family traditions mean so much to our children is that predictability makes them feel safe. Routines and rituals provide security at times of anxiety. They become an anchor of stability when the world seems a scary place. We can use everyday rituals to build calm, help our children register safety, and build trust and connection. These rituals don't have to be big things. They can be bedtime stories, building dens, favourite recipes, or family movie or board game nights. They help provide a sense of belonging, a sense of family, and a comforting rhythm to family life.

Family traditions are very individual and personal to each family, but taking the time to think about how we can connect with our children and strengthen family bonds is important.

☝ Give it a Try!

The Danes are known to be some of the happiest people in the world. This may well be linked to the concept of *Hygge* (pronounced hoo-geh) that families in Denmark practise. Hygge means creating a warm, cosy atmosphere and celebrating just being together. It often involves comfort food, drinks, blankets and cosying up together and is known to engender a feeling of wellbeing. As a family, it is about savouring the moment and taking time for connection. Autumn and Winter are known as the most Hygge time of year, as we wrap up and snuggle in front of the fire. However, we can make time as a family to create these moments at any time of year. It could be having a family movie night, a night in a homemade tent in the garden, a picnic in the park, a pyjama day, or making hot chocolate with marshmallows, which younger children would love. For older children, the concept is not only about the environment but also the philosophy. It is about creating a comforting social and emotional environment within our homes and an environment of safety, which should allow our children to relax and connect with us.

Finally, building a strong support network around your family will help you cope with the day-to-day stress of supporting a child who is struggling. This can include extended family members, friends, or, indeed, face-to-face or online support groups. Many parents report that their greatest support and understanding comes from others who are in the same position. Even if they may never have met in 'real life,' the validation and understanding of those in a similar situation can be invaluable in terms of emotional support and practical advice.

Self-Care

We have all heard the saying that a mother is only as happy as her least happy child. Well, when there is a child struggling with anxiety in the household, it impacts parental mental health. We always try to be the umbrella, taking some of the rain from our children. But we also need to remember to look after ourselves.

Let's re-consider the concepts of *One Good Adult* and *Scaffolding* our children and how we play an important role in supporting and guiding our children. When we think of scaffolding, we think of iron poles, pillars, and supports. It is strong, solid, and hard-wearing, offering safety and security. But to enable us to provide this strong and resilient framework for our children, we need to fortify ourselves first. If we are exhausted and distracted or on the verge of crashing to the ground ourselves, we will not be able to support others.

Give It a Try

In her book *Unraveling Motherhood*[49], Geraldine Walsh outlines an exercise that resonated with me in terms of better understanding all that mothers do and achieve in a day. I would highly recommend giving it a try. The task involves writing down two lists, she explains:

- List one: Begin by writing down the things you wanted to achieve today. Tick off the things you accomplished, which may be none.
- List two: Begin by writing down the first thing you did this morning [from getting up, making bed, dressing the kids….]. Then, write down the next thing you did, and the next, and so on. Continue to write down every task you accomplished throughout the day.
- Reflect: Look at your list and see how much you do in a single day. You are pretty amazing. Recognising this incredible list of things you do in that effortless way is not meant to exhaust us but rather highlight how necessary and important we are, how accomplished we are, and how we do so much more in one day than we ever imagined.

This task may also highlight just how much or how little you have done for your own emotional welfare during the day. She reminds us to have compassion for ourselves as women, not simply as mothers.

Psychologists often use the analogy of the *Exhaustion Funnel* when considering how we manage work and home life balance. Consider the image of a funnel to represent how we move from a balanced life to exhaustion. The widest point of the funnel represents a full and balanced life. This is when we have achieved a balance in our lives, a mixture of nourishing and depleting activities. These involve work, rest, and play. But, when times are tough, and our lives become overloaded, we start to let go of things – often the things that impact our wellbeing. We move down through the funnel. We begin by letting go of play, then rest. We often continue into a pattern that impacts our wellbeing. We lose the fun and joy in our lives and focus all our efforts on the struggle we are engaging with. This eventually leads to exhaustion and burnout.

☝ Give It a Try!

If you are feeling very stressed, it can sometimes help to focus on issues and solutions. It can help to identify your own individual stressors. Write down exactly what is bothering you. Make a list, and then rank the issues in order of severity. Even the act of putting the words on paper, being able to stand back from them and consider them in perspective, can help you gain clarity about what is causing you the most anxiety. Then, focus on your top three stressors. Brainstorm any ideas about what or who might help. Identifying specific stressors and considering possible solutions helps bring a feeling of control.

We have all heard the cabin crew say, 'In case of emergency, put your own oxygen mask on first before helping others.' This metaphor is often used for self-care in everyday life. But there is a major issue here. If we only consider self-care in the case of emergency, we will burn out. We need to reconsider time to care for ourselves now before physical, mental, and emotional anguish forces us to slow down. Don't wait for an emergency! Look after yourself now.

So, how do we address this and change it? An important first step is awareness. We need to tune into ourselves and notice when we start feeling exhausted. Watch for signs like not getting pleasure from things in life that you previously enjoyed, feeling that you are just going through the motions, and feeling more irritable and less patient with your family. If you notice changes like these on an ongoing basis, it is a sign that you need to pay attention to your wellbeing. Ask yourself:

- When did you last make time for yourself?
- When did you last take time to have fun with friends?
- When did you last read a book for pleasure?
- When did you last play?
- When did you last really belly laugh?
- When did you last take time in nature?
- When did you last dance?
- When did you last have breakfast in bed?
- When did you last spend time with your thoughts?

Our lives today are so much more frantic than in our parents and grandparents' time. This frenetic lifestyle impacts our parenting.

In his novel *Suzanne's Diary for Nicholas*, James Patterson uses a lovely analogy to highlight where our priorities should lie in balancing our family and work lives. He tells the reader to imagine life as a task where they are balancing five balls. These balls are called work, family, health, friendship, and integrity. You are juggling the five balls and keeping them all in the air. One day, you realise that work is a rubber ball. If you drop it, it bounces back. But the other four are made of glass. If you drop one of those, it will be irrevocably damaged. This reminds us to focus our energy on balancing the most precious aspects of our lives and worry less about work, which will always bounce back.

☝ Give it a Try!

Self-care can be such a personal thing. But here are a few things I would recommend considering to support your wellbeing:

- Human connection is a powerful antidote to stress. Make time to connect with someone supportive each day. This could be a phone call with a friend, a chat with a colleague over lunch, coffee with your partner, or a fun activity with your child.
- Commit to at least one wellbeing practice daily. This could be walking the dog, painting your nails, meditating, or going to the gym. No matter what each day holds, commit to one non-negotiable self-care item just for you.
- Prioritise your mental health over external pressures. When you are under real stress, practise the art of saying no to things that are not an absolute priority.
- Develop an attitude of gratitude. When we express gratitude, we shift our focus from what we don't have to what we do. Gratitude can be cultivated. One common practice is to keep a daily gratitude journal.
- Consider your social media usage. Social media can stop us from connecting with the ones we love. Switch off notifications with family/friends or keep the phone silent. Turn off your phone at night or keep your phone out of the bedroom. Have screen-free time before bed to improve quality of sleep. Don't check emails after hours. Let home time be home time.

Sometimes, to transform as adults, we need to let go of some of our old ideas. One of the ideas I feel many of us need to let go of is the idea of the perfect parent. A friend once told me that a perfect parent is like a Unicorn. We have all heard of them, but have you ever seen one? No. Because they don't actually exist!

This applies to mothers more than fathers. We put ourselves under pressure to constantly strive to meet the never-ending societal expectations of motherhood. We are sold the lie that responsible motherhood is near to martyrdom. Instead, we need to model the behaviour we would like our children to follow. If we want them to understand the value of self-care, we need to show them a mother who does the same.

👍 Give it a Try!

In his book *Essentialism: The Disciplined Pursuit of Less*, Greg McKeown speaks about the insidious idea of trying to do it all. Instead, he recommends living life with the aim of focusing on the disciplined pursuit of less. He argues that we need to figure out what is most important in our lives, eliminate the trivial, and focus on the most important areas. To do this, we also need to learn to say no. This can be so hard for many of us. But McKeown argues that learning to be more selective in our pursuits is an essential aspect of our lives. He recommends the following one-minute strategy for learning to say no:

- Evaluate the opportunity. Ask yourself if you will feel bad about saying no to this opportunity a year from now.
- Focus on the trade-off. Ask yourself what else will you have to give up if you say yes to the opportunity,
- Remember what it feels like to say no. Ask yourself how it felt last time you said no to an opportunity that wasn't right for you.

If you are anything like me, you may well feel a great sense of relief after you have said no to something that was just going to eat into precious time that could be spent with your family or, indeed, time for self-care.

If we consider the core components of self-compassion, what does it involve? It should include self-kindness and a sense of care and understanding for ourselves, just as we would show for a friend. It should also involve an understanding that we are all imperfect. We can develop an awareness of how we judge ourselves and those feelings of not being good enough. Most of us have a loud, self-critical inner voice, and we don't take the time to acknowledge the pain of self-judgement. If we are to find the strength to support our children, we need to first stop and show ourselves a little compassion.

One of the defining characteristics of being human is being flawed, and an acceptance that we are all perfectly imperfect allows us to show more self-compassion. As parents, so many of us are so hard on ourselves. I think that is even more so when our children are struggling. The tendency to blame ourselves or consider our responses very harshly can be hard to move beyond. So, instead of letting our self-criticism take over our thoughts, consider how we can show ourselves a little more self-compassion in that moment.

The language we use towards ourselves can make such a difference. If we are struggling to cope, instead of belittling ourselves, we can replace that thought with a more self-compassionate one. I am doing the best I can at this moment. If we respond to our child in a way that we regret, instead of berating ourselves for failing our child, we can remind ourselves that we made a mistake and will try to learn from it and do better next time. Just as I suggested that children struggling with anxiety can ask themselves what they would tell a friend in the same position, we, as parents, can do the same. When we stop to consider the compassionate response we would give a friend in the same position, it can be a good reminder of how harsh we can be towards ourselves at times of difficulty.

Engaging With the System

One of the important things to remember, and I have mentioned it previously, is that there is a danger that we consider anxiety to be an endpoint for our children or teens. They are forever to be known as 'our anxious child.' Although for many of our children, anxiety is something they will have to deal with on an ongoing basis, the important thing is that they don't just accept it as a 'diagnosis' of who they are. It is something they are dealing with, not a personality trait. Often, external support can assist us in helping our children to move beyond those anxious feelings.

A Word to the Wise

'I truly believe, in all honesty, that we all have a screw loose. Nobody's perfectly mentally stable. It's not possible. But some of us are just in a better place than others. Sometimes, like an engine, a fan belt wears thin. A head gasket builds up pressure over time. A gearbox gets worn down. An engine needs care and consideration, and when it's not looked after, a professional must intervene. The mind is the same. Sometimes, in our lifetime, we may need a qualified mechanic to step in and fit this complex combustion chamber that they call the brain. It's amazing how the right help can change everything.'

Credit: Conor Nolan, Author of *Normal*[50]

As the public conversation about anxiety becomes more prominent and awareness has reduced the stigma associated with mental health difficulties, you would expect support also to increase. However, even though there is greater recognition of the impact of anxiety, and it is a word that is very familiar to both children and teenagers today, levels of funding for the support required have not caught up with public consciousness.

Learning From Psychology

Research has highlighted the growing mental health crisis among children and teenagers across the world.

In Ireland, demand for Child and Adolescent Mental Health Services (CAMHS) increased by a third between 2020 and 2021. In 2023, the Health Services Executive report that some children are waiting up to two years for an appointment.

Similarly, in the UK, the Royal College of Paediatrics and Child Health reported in May 2023 that waiting lists for mental health support are the highest since records began. More than 400,000 children are on mental health waiting lists, an increase of almost 40% in just two years.

The American Psychological Association have also reported surging demands for mental health care since the COVID-19 pandemic. As cases of anxiety, depression and mood disorders increase, a survey of their members in 2022 found that 60% of psychologists reported no openings for new patients.

Although your child may be referred through the public system, long delays are often experienced. The consequences of such long waitlists are particularly damaging for children. The importance of early intervention is constantly highlighted when considering the needs of young children. These prolonged delays impact older children and teens as well, in terms of their mental health, their education, and overall wellbeing. However, once seen, a therapist or clinical psychologist can successfully treat most children.

Parents often seek out private support while waiting on the public system. When seeking professional support privately, I would always advise you to find someone with proper accreditation, for example, a Chartered Psychologist who is registered with an authorising body such as the Psychological Society of Ireland (PSI), British Psychological Society (BPS) or the American Psychological Association (APA). There are several ways you can find a Chartered Psychologist in your area. Your first port of call is often your GP, who can help and guide you. But organisations like the three above have online directories where you can search for someone with the qualifications you need in your local area.

Equally, child and adolescent psychotherapists are trained mental health professionals qualified to work with children and adolescents and their families. They aim to look beneath the surface of difficult emotions and behaviours, paying close attention not only to the views of the child or adolescent but also through non-verbal communication and behaviour. They help children and adolescents to understand themselves and their problems, making sense of their experiences, thoughts, and feelings. Research has shown that such therapy can be very effective in the treatment of anxiety disorders. Again, when seeking a counsellor or psychotherapist for your child or teen, it is best to check credentials and membership of an accredited body.

For some children, particularly younger ones, play therapy can be very effective. Play therapy helps children to make sense of their world, and research has shown it can be very effective for children with emotional issues, communication difficulties, relationship issues, children who have experienced bereavement or loss, and children struggling with anxiety. Play therapy uses a variety of playful activities to meet each individual child's needs. As play is the language of children, it enables them to bring into focus emotions which they are unable to verbalise. It can help children better understand their thoughts and feelings and work through difficult life experiences. According to the professional organisation Play Therapy International, play therapy results in positive change for 70% of children who experience it. Once again, it is best to enquire about training credentials and accreditation when seeking professional support.

There are various other child-friendly therapies that can be effective in supporting a child in exploring their emotions. Music therapy, art therapy, and drama therapy are a few. Many children will find expressing their feelings visually easier than talking about them. Many children will struggle to talk about their fears and may find it very challenging to express their emotions. These therapies provide a conduit through which children can start to express these emotions in different ways.

Although sometimes it can be daunting to think of engaging with professionals, remember that professional support can be life-changing for your child. There are times in life when we need support or advice from those with training and experience in the field of psychology. However, remember that you know your child better than anyone else, and that includes professionals. No matter what type of support you engage to work with you and your family, you should be an equal partner in the process.

Conclusion

Mild to moderate anxiety can be a part of life for many children at points during their childhood. However, if your child's anxiety is persistent and impacts their everyday life, it could be considered clinical, and they may need further one-to-one support. Please remember that this does not, in any way, mean you are failing as a parent. It just means that sometimes your child might need individualised input from a professional with the training and experience to explore issues in more depth.

Please always seek support if your child's anxiety
is something they have been struggling with for more than
three months,
and is a problem that is significantly affecting their daily life.

A psychologist or accredited therapist can help your child work through ongoing issues and develop a personalised plan of action to better manage their anxiety.

However, if I have one last message to give, it is to remember that YOU are the most important tool you have in your toolbox to support your child struggling with anxiety. This is true even when availing of professional support. It is our love and connection, our family bond, and being a positive influence in their lives that will help them flourish.

A Final Word

Every parent feels under pressure at times to be a perfect parent. Society puts us under pressure, and we put ourselves under pressure, too. We are not 'perfect' parents because our children are doing well, nor are we 'bad' parents because our children are struggling. So often, when our children are under pressure, we beat ourselves up wondering what past misdemeanour of ours may have caused their difficulties. There are so many ways in which we try to blame ourselves. Just because your child may be having a difficult time does not make you a bad parent. Many of us need to hear this and start our journey to support our children by reminding ourselves that this is the truth. We are doing our best for our children, and that is what matters.

Now that you are equipped with tools and guidance, you will better understand your child's anxiety, the impact of the brain on their body, and techniques which will help you to support them. The approaches outlined in this book are intended to help you assist your child, whether you are happy to deal with their anxiety yourself or are waiting for professional support.

So, what are the steps ahead, having read these pages? I encourage you to start by talking to your child about their anxiety. Explain the causes and get them to consider the symptoms they are living with.

Let them become familiar with the amygdala, the body's internal alarm system. As you normalise anxiety, remind them that it is something they can overcome. Understanding how anxiety works in the brain and impacts the body is the first step in understanding how the various treatment methods work. Remind them that every time they engage in deep breathing or use any self-regulation tool, their brains are changing. They are teaching their brain how to respond to challenging situations.

Then, work on building ladders. Every time they step outside their comfort zone, remind them that they are strengthening the pathways in their brains that help them to be brave in the face of distress. Remind them that safety does not mean the absence of any threat. Safety is knowing you have the skill sets and the supportive relationships to help you deal with them.

As parents, the overwhelming instinct when our children are struggling is to support them. However, in doing so, we often accommodate the anxious feelings. It is important that we find our inner strength if we want our children to find theirs. Instead of constantly jumping in to 'save' them, we want to validate their fears and encourage bravery. Remember, the task at hand is not to try to make the anxiety go away. Instead, it is to support our children to feel stronger and more capable of dealing with it when it comes.

When working on finding their inner bravery, there may be days that you will feel you have taken a step backwards. But be reassured that the time you spend teaching your child new skills can be life changing. The results are worth the effort you put in. If you have had a particularly tough day, take a moment at the end of the day to remind your child and yourself that you will pick yourselves up and try again tomorrow. The most important thing is to be gentle to yourself and gentle to your child and keep taking baby steps forward.

We cannot promise they will never face challenging situations, but we can let them see our faith in their ability to cope. Reminding them of their internal strength will encourage them to see it, too, while equipping them with tools to help them be brave when they don't feel it. With our support, they can find their inner strength and achieve all we know they are capable of.

There is an old Indian proverb about a Cherokee Indian Chief and his grandson. He tells his grandson that life is a battle between two wolves inside us. The first wolf is *Fear*. It brings with it anxiety, uncertainty, hesitancy, and indecision. The second wolf is *Faith*. It brings calm, confidence, decisiveness, and action. 'But which wolf will win, grandfather?' the grandson asks. His grandfather replies, 'The one we feed.'

Our children who struggle with anxiety need to learn to have faith in themselves. Faith in their ability to live their lives to the full. Faith in their ability to stretch outside their comfort zones. Faith that they can leave the safe harbour and follow their hopes and dreams.

Endnotes

[1] Tronick, E., et al., (1975) *Infant Emotions in Normal and Pertubated Interactions.* Paper presented at the biennial meeting of the Society for Research in Child Development, Denver, CO

[2] Gergely, A., Koós-Hutás, É., Filep, L.A. et al. (2023) Six facial prosodic expressions caregivers similarly display to infants and dogs. *Sci Rep* 13, 929.

[3] Bowlby, J., (1969) *Attachment and Loss, Vol. 1: Attachment.* New York: Basic Books

[4] Winnicott, D., (1971) *Playing and Reality.* New York: Basic Books

[5] Jigsaw/UCD (2019) *My World 2 Survey.* Available at: http://www.myworldsurvey.ie/

[6] Coyne, M., (2020) *Love In, Love Out: A Compassionate Approach to Parenting Your Anxious Child.* London: Harper Collins Press

[7] Benton, T. D., et al., (2021) *Addressing the Global Crisis of Child and Adolescent Mental Health. JAMA Pediatrics.* 175(11):1108–1110

[8] National Health Service (2020) *Mental Health of Children and Young People in England.* NHS Digital

[9] The Children's Society (2022) *The Good Childhood Report*, London: The Children's Society

[10] Australian Bureau of Statistics (2022) *National Study of Mental Health and Wellbeing.* Available at: https://www.abs.gov.au/statistics/health/mental-health/national-study-mental-health-and-wellbeing/2020-21

[11] Cannon, M., et al., (2013) *The Mental Health of Young People in Ireland: a report of the Psychiatric Epidemiology Research across the Lifespan.* Dublin: Royal College of Surgeons in Ireland

[12] Bergeron, L., (2013) *Size, connectivity of brain region linked to anxiety level in young children, study shows.* Available at: https://med.stanford.edu/news/all-news/2013/11/size-connectivity-of-brain-region-linked-to-anxiety-level-in-young-children-study-shows.html

[13] Cuddy, Amy J.C., Caroline A. Wilmuth, and Dana R. Carney. (2012) *"The Benefit of Power Posing Before a High-Stakes Social Evaluation."* Harvard Business School Working Paper, No. 13-027, September 2012.

[14] Jungmann, M, Vencatachellum, S, Van Ryckeghem, D, Vögele, C. (2018) Effects of Cold Stimulation on Cardiac-Vagal Activation in Healthy Participants: Randomized Controlled Trial. *JMIR Form Res.* 2018 Oct 9;2(2).

[15] Chiang, C.T. et al. (2010) The effect of ice water ingestion on autonomic modulation in healthy subjects. *Clin Auton Res.* 2010 Dec;20(6):375-80.

[16] Lucy Nathanson, Child Therapist and Expert in Selective Mutism. Available at: https://www.confidentchildren.co.uk/

[17] Dr Niall Neeson, the *Dental Fear Solutions Programme* at Boyne Dental, Instagram @thecalmingdentist

[18] Leahy, Robert. L. (2006) *The Worry Cure: Stop Worrying and Start Living*. London: Piatkus

[19] The Woodland Trust (2023) Anxiety is Soaring Due to Lack of Access to Green Space. Available at: https://www.woodlandtrust.org.uk/press-centre/2023/03/young-people-climate-anxiety-green-space-access/

[20] Alex Koster, Author of the Training Course *Hope and Empowerment through Mindful Nature Connection* Instagram @rootsandwingsecotherapy

[21] Tara Shannon, Author of the *Rabbit and Bear* books. Available at: https://www.tarashannonwrites.com/

[22] Taren, A., et al., (2013) *Dispositional Mindfulness Co-Varies with Smaller Amygdala and Caudate Volumes in Community Adults*. Available at: https://journals.plos.org/plosone/article?id=10.1371/journal.pone.0064574

[23] Bolte Taylor, J., (2006) *My Stroke of Insight: A Brain Scientist's Personal Journey*. New York: Penguin Press

[24] Schultchen, Dana et al (2019). Effects of an 8-Week Body Scan Intervention on Individually Perceived Psychological Stress and Related Steroid Hormones in Hair. *Mindfulness*. 10.10.1007/s12671-019-01222-7.

[25] Louise Shanagher, founder of *Creative Mindfulness Kids*. Available at: https://www.creative-mindfulness.com/home

[26] Dr Katie Hurley, Author, Speaker, Child and Adolescent Mental Health Expert. Available at: https://practicalkatie.com/about-me/

[27] Cohen, L. J., (2013) *The Opposite of Worry: The Playful Parenting Approach to Childhood Anxieties and Fears*. New York: Ballantine Books

[28] Hammoud, R. *et al.* (2022) Smartphone-based ecological momentary assessment reveals mental health benefits of birdlife. *Sci Rep* 12, 17589.

[29] Stobbe, E., Sundermann, J., *et al.* (2022) Birdsongs alleviate anxiety and paranoia in healthy participants. *Sci Rep* 12, 16414.

[30] Hardy, D., (2012) *The Compound Effect*. CDS Books.

[31] Tara Shannon, Author of the *Rabbit and Bear* books. Available at: https://www.tarashannonwrites.com/

[32] Emery, S., (1978) *Actualizations: You Don't Have to Rehearse to Be Yourself*. Random House Inc.

[33] Cohen, L. J., (2013) *The Opposite of Worry: The Playful Parenting Approach to Childhood Anxieties and Fears*. New York: Ballantine Books

[34] Lebowitz, E., (2019) *Addressing Parental Accommodation When Treating Anxiety in Children*, New York: Oxford University Press

[35] Curran, T., and Hill, A. P., (2019). *Perfectionism is increasing over time: A meta-analysis of birth cohort differences from 1989 to 2016. Psychological Bulletin, 145*(4): 410–429. https://doi.org/10.1037/bul0000138

[36] Twenge, J., (2018) *iGen: Why Today's Super-Connected Kids Are Growing Up Less Rebellious, More Tolerant, Less Happy--and Completely Unprepared for Adulthood--and What That Means for the Rest of Us*. US: Simon and Schuster.

[37] Elkind, D., (2011) Can We Play? In *Too Much Too Soon: Early learning and the erosion of childhood* Ed House, R., United Kingdom: Hawthorn Press

[38] Leo, P., (2005) *Connection Parenting: Parenting Through Connection Instead of Coercion, Through Love Instead of Fear*. Oregon: Wyatt MacKenzie Publishing Inc.

[39] Shumacker, H., (2018) *It's OK to Go Up the Slide : Renegade Rules for Raising Confident and Creative Kids*. UK: Penguin Publishing Group.

[40] Dodd, H., (2023) *Child's Play: Examining the Association Between Time Spent Playing and Child Mental Health. Child Psychiatry and Human Development*. 54: 1678-1686 *Available at:* https://link.springer.com/article/10.1007/s10578-022-01363-2

[41] Rotter, J.B., (1996) Generalised expectancies of internal versus external control of reinforcement. *Psychological Monographs*, 80 (1): 1-28

[42] Twenge, J., (2004) It's Beyond My Control: A Cross Temporal Meta-Analysis of Increasing Externality of Locus of Control. *Journal of Personality and Social Psychology*. 8 (3): 308-19

[43] Blackwell, L.S., Trzesniewski, K.H., Dweck, C.S., (2007). Implicit theories of intelligence predict achievement across an adolescent transition: a longitudinal study and an intervention. Child Dev. 2007 Jan-Feb;78(1):246-63.

[44] Overbye, K., Bøen, R., Huster, R.J. and Tamnes, C.K., (2020) Learning From Mistakes: How Does the Brain Handle Errors?. *Frontiers for Young Minds*. 8:80.

[45] Ward, K., *Kisses from Boys* Available at: https://www.instagram.com/kissesfromboys/

[46] In my first book *Perfectly Imperfect Parenting: Connection Not Perfection*, I have discussed the role of technology in our children's lives to a greater extent. Available at: https://www.drmaryokane.ie/perfectly-imperfect-parenting/

[47] Haidt, J., (2023) *Social Media is Taking a Dangerous Toll on Teenage Girls*. The New Statesman. Available at: https://www.newstatesman.com/technology/2023/03/jonathan-haidt-social-media-dangerous-teenage-girls-anxiety-depression

[48] Kelly, Y., Zilanawala, A., Booker, C., Sacker, A., (2019) Social Media Use and Adolescent Mental Health: Findings From the UK Millennium Cohort Study. *EClinicalMedicine*. 2019 Jan 4;6:59-68.

[49] Walsh, G., (2023) Unraveling Motherhood: Understanding Your Experience through Self-Reflection, Self-Care&Authenticity. Hatherleigh Press. Available at: https://gutterbookshop.com/product/unraveling-motherhood-by-geraldine-walsh/

[50] Nolan, C., (2020) *Normal*. Instagram: @Conor_N7. Book available at: https://www.amazon.co.uk/Normal-Conor-Nolan/dp/1913704602

Acknowledgements

Before I start to thank the various people who have contributed to the making of this book, I would like to start with a few words of gratitude to my three wonderful children who have made me the person I am today. I would never claim to have this motherhood thing fully sorted, but they have taught me so much over the years. As they have grown, I have grown along with them. They have challenged my thinking, my perspective on life, and my patience! They have changed my priorities, and taught me so much about life, love, and about myself. I am still very much a work in progress, but each one of them has most definitely made me a better person. Thank you to Erin, Michael, and Kira xxx.

Thanks to my editor, Geraldine Walsh, who has once again been such a support throughout the writing of this book. I thought that writing a second book would be easier than the first. Oops! But once again, Ger stopped me in my tracks, and helped me to really find my own voice when writing. Ger, you have no idea how good you are at what you do.

Thanks to Jeremy Murphy at JM Agency, Publishing Consultancy for his professionalism throughout the publishing process. He made the process very easy. Thanks also to Parvathi Venkitaraman of JM

Agency for the wonderful cover and book design. I had a very clear vision of what I wanted on the cover, so thank you for your patience in working to bring that concept to life.

I would also like to thank Frank Kelly, Brian Colleran and all the team at Lettertec Ireland Ltd for printing this edition of the book to an exceptional standard and for using the best in both craft and digital printing technology.

Thanks to Alexandra Koster, Lucy Nathanson, Niall Neeson, and Louise Shanagher for their 'Ask the Expert' input. Thanks also to all of those who gave permission to use quotations from their work in my book: Dr Malie Coyne, Dr Katie Hurley, Conor Nolan, Tara Shannon, Mark Smyth, and Krista Ward.

Thank you so much to Anton Savage for writing the Foreword. It is always an absolute pleasure to speak to you on The Anton Savage Show on Newstalk Radio. Our chats could never be considered work! Thanks also to Tommy Bowe, Dr David Coleman, Alison Curtis, Allison Keating, Karen Koster, Dave Moore, Niamh Fitzpatrick and Mairead Ronan for taking the time to read advance copies and sending through such wonderful reviews.

Finally thank you to all the family and friends who have supported me over the past few years. Especially Liam, my mum, Gemma and Aideen. Beany and Cathy, and my walking buddies Joan and Isabel.

About the Author

Dr Mary O'Kane is a Lecturer in Psychology and Early Childhood Studies at the Open University. Her research interests include childhood transitions; self esteem and wellbeing, and the value of play. She is an expert contributor to the Anton Savage Show on Newstalk radio discussing a broad range of parenting and childhood issues while also responding to viewers' parenting queries. She is also a regular contributor to various other national and local media outlets. Her first book *Perfectly Imperfect Parenting: Connection Not Perfection* was published in April 2021, and received an Honorary Mention in the Eric Hoffer Book Awards. She gives public talks and online Webinars for parents and educators on a range of topics related to child wellbeing, parenting, and education. For more information on her work see www.drmaryokane.ie or you can follow her on social media.

Printed in Great Britain
by Amazon

49807771R00138